Empty Nest

Strategies To Help Your Kids Take Flight

Marci Seither

SAWMILL PRESS

To my husband, John.
After three-plus decades of marriage, six kids, and an armload
of the cutest grandbabies this side of the Mississippi, I still love
lingering over a cup of coffee with you in the morning.

I am so thankful for all your support and encouragement in the
good times and through the tight ring years. Looking forward
to new adventures together.

CONTENTS

1

REMEMBER TO BREATHE

Well, lose a daughter . . . gain an office!" my dad jokingly said when I moved out.

He was kidding as usual, but I think it really masked the pain of saying good-bye. Not just to the child who was moving out of her room with the daisy wallpaper, but to everything else, such as daily interaction, family dinners, and all the traditions that we wrap around our families.

Sometimes it is so hard to put into words what we are really feeling because often we don't know what we are feeling ourselves. There is silent mourning. It is parents' rite of passage as they wit-ness their children stretch their wings at the edge of the nest and finally lift off.

The cycle continues from one generation to the next. Before I knew it, I helplessly looked on as my kids began to box up some of their items. Some they planned to take and others were put into the attic. Clothes were packed away, leaving empty dresser drawers that still smelled like snowboard wax and fabric softener. For the first time I thought about all the gray-haired women who stopped me in the grocery store as I tried consoling a cranky toddler.

"These are the best years," they would smile with a far-off look in their eyes. "They go by so quickly, so cherish them while you can." Then they shuffled away, leaving me standing there with a blank stare and smelling a lot like peanut butter and baby wipes. I looked like a wrinkle bomb had exploded within my kill zone. I had no idea what they were talking about. Now I fully understand because in their wisdom they were right.

Anyone who has kids who have left home or will soon leave home knows that those words of wisdom are true. And now I find myself tell-ing the same thing to young moms . . . only without the gray hair, thanks to L'Oreal Mocha Medium Brown, and without the shuffle.

HOW TO FOCUS—AND HOW TO BREATHE

I have no idea what all the unfocused breathers did before the official term "pant-blow" became part of the natural birth vocabulary. No one mentions the two major Lamaze class points during other medical endeavors. I have yet to hear my dentist ask, "How would you like a natural root canal?" or "Maybe you should find a focal point before we start doing your filling." Yeah, I would find a focal point. It would be the bright "exit" sign right over the door. For anyone who has had the experience of being in a birthing class, you know that breathing and focusing are esteemed as an art form.

About three months after our marriage, John came home from work one evening to find a surprise when he opened the freezer section of our small refrigerator.

"Honey," he asked, wondering if it may have something to do with my part-time job working at a preschool. "What is up with all the boxes of juice bars in the freezer?"

"Oh," I responded. "I was out shopping and they just sounded so refreshing, so I picked some up."

"Three boxes for two people?" he asked. "Mmm."

The next morning when the thought of finishing my first cup of coffee began to gag me, we instantly knew we weren't just two people living in our one-bedroom apartment.

"Maybe you should take a pregnancy test," he suggested.

Those were before the days of home pregnancy tests, so I made an appointment and went in then went home and waited for the nurse to call with the results. The next day I was informed that I had passed with flying colors!

A follow-up appointment was made, and I joined the ranks of a new group. I was officially a mother-to-be.

After being weighed and measured I was sent home again, only this time with a cute diaper bag, compliments of a baby formula company, a small bale of coupons for items I might need in the near future, and a large book titled *What to Expect When You're Expecting.* I read and reread the book several times during that first trimester in between experiencing another term I quickly learned: morning sickness.

Before we knew it, we were enrolled in a natural birthing class with a room full of pregnant women and their coaches. John practiced rubbing my lower back with a tennis ball. I was starting to fill out the bright-colored maternity tops that looked like they were made for gigantic Oompa Loompas, and both of us were pretty anxious as my due date approached.

From the rafters over my parents' garage we retrieved the old wicker bassinet that had already cradled two generations. Lovingly we scrubbed it, and my grandmother sewed new bedding. Then we added a soft blanket and a cuddly windup bear that played lullabies. The diaper bag and my overnight case were packed and ready to grab at the first twinges of labor.

The feeling of having your bag carefully packed and ready to take to the hospital is a stark contrast to watching your child pack his or her own bag and leave home without you.

I was so thankful to have nine months to prepare for bringing our first baby into the world. How odd it is that we often don't have that luxury of time and undivided attention to prepare our hearts when it is time to release them into the world.

TIME TO FIND A FOCAL POINT

Breathing is something we do naturally. It can also be something we do intentionally, so find a focal point. For the first nine months they needed you to help them grow and depended on you for oxygen. Little lungs expanded, followed by the sweetest sound of your baby's first cry.

Just like the day they were born, soon it will be time to push them out and cut the umbilical cord. Only this time it is often the parents who need oxygen to breathe through this natural transition from one stage of parenting to the next.

When the big bird feathers of adulthood crowd through the whisper-soft down of adolescence, it is time to focus on where they want to soar, not on where you want them to stay. Focusing on what's important is not always easy since it involves emotions we haven't dealt with before.

HYPERVENTILATING HAPPENS

I wasn't surprised when Nathan expressed interest in enlisting in the Marine Corps; I just wasn't expecting such a huge announcement to be made at the dinner table. But that is what happened, proof that life can change in a matter of moments. Even though Nathan's decision was based on a lot of well-gathered information, prayer, and discussion, I wasn't ready for it to be so final. So abrupt. And especially not between dinner and blackberry picking, which we would often do on warm summer nights. Then we'd top off the blackberries with a scoop of vanilla ice cream.

"Tomorrow, after I go wakeboarding with my friends," Nathan said as he stood up to clear his plate, "I am going to the recruiter's office to finish up the paperwork I need to join the Marines." I looked at him in shock and then at my husband. John was totally calm, which was fine because I had enough adrenaline for a whole squadron of parents.

"What?" was my not-so-collected response. I looked at Nathan and then back at John, my eyes popping out like my parents' pet Pugs. "Do something! Call someone! Blackberry picking is canceled!" I am not always the most rational when I get upset, but at least I am big enough to admit it.

My reaction wasn't really about Nathan doing what I knew he wanted to do or going where he felt he needed to go. It was about me. I had been the maker of grilled cheese sandwiches and the keeper of childhood traditions like making homemade Play-Doh on rainy days and teaching the kids how to make mazes on the driveway with sidewalk chalk. Now, I was feeling displaced, vulnerable, and no longer needed. I wasn't ready for things to change in our family. Nathan was ready to leave the nest; I just wasn't ready to let him go.

Nathan wasn't the only one ready to stretch out his wings. Emma was right behind him. She had contemplated doing a foreign exchange program her senior year, but after looking into it we realized that she really needed only one more semester of high school credits to graduate. John's sister Beth had been a teacher in Saipan for the last twenty years, so Emma decided to graduate early and head for the small Micronesia island for a six-month cultural exchange with Beth and her family.

BUCKLE YOUR SEATBELTS—YOU MAY EXPERIENCE TURBULENCE AHEAD!

The week before Emma left for the other side of the globe, one of her friends flew in for a visit. Life was hectic as plans and packing consumed our time and energy. The day I took Emma's friend back to the airport, I hit unexpected turbulence.

I figured I might as well talk to the airline clerk while we were there and ask about luggage restrictions for overseas flights. I stepped up to the counter and when he looked up and asked, "Can I help you?" I totally lost focus and began to hyperventilate. I didn't know whether to look for a Kleenex or a paper bag.

"My child is leaving . . . for Saipan." I started to hiccup and gasp at the same time. He frantically began checking his screen, typing as fast as he could on the keyboard. A confused look came over his face. Emma rolled her eyes in embarrassment, stepped back, and hoped the security camera would not be able to identify us as being together.

"Ma'am," the kind man stated, still staring at the screen. "I am not showing we have any flights to Saipan this afternoon."

I caught my breath and through blurred eyes stammered, "She doesn't leave for ten days."

I am sure that at that point he pulled up the calendar and put in a request for vacation days. He probably had visions of a half-crazed mother on the edge running across the tarmac for one last wave good-bye and holding a pan of still-warm brownies yelling, "Wait! She forgot her snack!"

Crazy, yes, but I am sure I am not the only mother who has had to refrain herself when her child goes past the checkpoint at an airport.

I should have found a new focal point and remembered to breathe. And in case of extreme emergencies, you might want to carry along a paper bag for hyperventilation.

NOT ALONE

When I mentioned to a friend that I was considering writing about this topic her response was, "Hurry, I need it now!"

I knew Jenny and Joel before they had kids. Jenny's first career choice when she became pregnant with their first child, Taylor, was to be a full-time, stay-at-home mom. Now Taylor is going into her senior year at high school and filling out college applications. Taylor leaving the nest is something that will be a reality too soon for Jenny.

"You are what I do!" Jenny told Taylor. "You are my career, and I feel like I'm being forced into retirement without consent."

"I'm really proud of her, but it feels awful," stated Jenny. "I always have something going to keep me busy, plus we have two other kids, but knowing how fast the time flies makes this transition even harder."

Jenny knows that having her oldest daughter move out of the house isn't the end of their relationship, but she, like many other parents, isn't ready for their lives to be different.

"I love our family traditions," continued Jenny. "Everything from pumpkin carving to decorating the Christmas tree is special. I know that it will not be the same because from now on, someone will always be missing."

For Jenny and other moms who have had the opportunity to choose motherhood as their first career, being outsourced is a natural occupational reality. The thought that things will never be the same is hard for the active mom who savors family traditions.

Sometimes in an attempt to console, people would tell me, "You still have kids at home." But that doesn't change the fact that someone is leaving. And things will not be the same. Because we have such a big family, we made sure that our table could easily be expanded to accommodate our family plus a handful of guests. Now passing plates around an empty table feels so disconnected. Vacant spaces where our kids sat are a daily reminder that they have not just gone away for a few days. Finally I took action. I removed one of the leaves from the table, a visual acknowledgment that our family was really getting smaller and needed to adjust.

Although my dad used to joke about gaining an office, I realized that my departure must have felt similar to my parents. For myself, it was hard to know that I would never live there again in the same way but comforting to know that I always had a home to come back to. We can give that comfort to our kids as well.

We can always add an extra leaf or two back into the table for extra seating when everyone comes home.

HOLDING OUR BREATH

I hate needles. I don't know what it is about them that makes me weak in the knees, but they do. In fact a few years ago in an attempt to get over the fear, I actually donated blood. Knowing that it would help someone else helped . . . a little. I didn't even tell my family I was going to the blood drive until after I donated, just in case I backed out, or worse, got sick to my stomach: a realistic fear since it wouldn't have been the first time.

I had just gotten my pregnancy results when the doctor's office had me come in for a full screening, which included giving up several vials of my blood. The smell of the rubbing alcohol on the cotton ball caused me to suck up my air, and as the nurse gently swapped the inside crook of my elbow, I began to feel a little like I was on a very small boat on a very large ocean. The nurse started moving side to side, and the room tilted. Sweat sprang out from places I didn't even know had sweat glands.

"Are you going to pass out?" the nurse asked, as she loosened the elastic band around my upper arm.

"No," I weakly replied. "I am just going to throw up." And I did—all over the nurse, the table, and the paperwork.

"We need a wheelchair in here!" she said, holding my hand with one of hers and protecting the blood samples with the other.

I was a mess! Literally. And so was the nurse. They sat me in the waiting room until my color returned to something that didn't resemble paste and asked if there was someone who could come and drive me home. I was mortified as I sipped on the 7UP some-one brought out to me. Yikes. For years after that I was even more afraid of needles, thinking it was the blood test that made me sick, but after playing that almost comical scene over and over in my mind, I realized my problem wasn't the original fear. It was the fact that I had been holding my breath. Holding my breath.

From that time on as soon as I sit down to have blood drawn, I find a focal point and breathe. It doesn't mean I love needles now, but it makes shots of any kind or donating blood totally doable.

Remembering to breathe doesn't make saying good-bye to our kids any easier, but it helps us to not allow our fears to become bigger than they need to be.

Just to prove I could get over my silly fear, I decided to sign up to donate blood the next time I saw a local blood drive. I focused, remembered to breathe, and got the T-shirt!

FOCUS DOESN'T MEAN FIXATE

I floated the idea out to my Facebook friends that sometimes we as parents get so fixated on the problem and pain, we forget to breathe and focus. I asked my friends what they did to help them in times of distress.

Their responses were awesome. Their advice boiled down to the same things we learned in Lamaze class, only now the impor-tance was on *refocusing*.

Instead of fixating on the issue at hand, take a step back, com-mit it to the Lord, and take a moment to breathe in a big fresh cleansing breath that produces a wave of relaxation. Pray. And fo-cus on the things that are true by singing the comforting hymns that carry the messages of hope we have in Christ.

The Lord cares about the anxieties we face. He wants to help us overcome those times when we feel like we are stuck in the thick of emotional turmoil.

WORDS OF WISDOM

I asked friend and licensed marriage family therapist Kate Piper what she would tell parents who are facing times of stress concerning their child leaving home. She advised them to ask themselves:

1. How did you envision this part of your life when you thought about it five years ago? For you? For your child? For your spouse?
2. What are the fears you have for you and your child leading up to the time when your child actually leaves?
3. What is the legacy you want for this moment? Not from your lips but from your actions to your child? Get clear about the message you want to send. This is a memory milestone that you child will recall forever. Just like when we hated going for that first vaccine or to the dentist, we had to set our worries aside and put a calm face on. That applies in this case, maybe even more so. Also, think about the blessing you would like to give to your child.

Further, Piper advises parents:

1. **Call a friend** to pray with you, laugh with you, and cry with you. Let friends "carry [your] burdens" through this. Someday you will need to be that friend for someone else.
2. **Breathe deeply.** Use a technique called square breathing. Breathe in through your nose for four counts; hold your breath for four counts; breathe out through your mouth for four counts, and rest while your breath is out for four counts. Repeat four times.

If all else fails and you don't think you can hold the tears and fear any longer, get your child an earring or nose ring piercing (which, incidentally, has a GPS tracker installed). That way, you won't be surprised when your child confess what he or she actually did with that college money you sent.

Okay, maybe not, but you get the picture.

I waited patiently for the LORD; he turned to me and heard my cry. He lifted me out of the slimy pit, out of the mud and mire; he set my feet on a rock and gave me a firm place to stand. He put a new song in my mouth, a hymn of praise to our God. Many will see and fear the LORD and put their trust in him. Psalm 40:1-3

Reflections

List five things you can do this week that will help you remember
to breathe and relax, such as:

- Call a friend you haven't talked to in a
  while.
- Take a walk.
- Listen to music.
- Doodle using colored pencils.

"The best and most beautiful things in the World cannot be seen or even touched ~ they must be felt with the heart.

Helen Keller

2

CHANGING SEASONS

I'm from California but for nine years we lived in Minnesota. I did not expect the culture shock. The first time I went to the grocery store to get fresh basil, they asked where I came from. Up to that point I had never considered Jell-O with fruit cocktail, marshmallows, topped with a dollop of Cool Whip a salad. The thought of adding spam, cream of mushroom soup, string beans, and tater tots together in a casserole dish never crossed my mind. I learned that being invited over for "lunch" was much different from having a sandwich, some fruit, and a handful of chips. And the one-finger waves exchanged between drivers in Minnesota had a totally different meaning than the one-finger waves exchanged between drivers on a busy California interstate.

The winters were harsh and cold, but the people were warm and endearing.

Even though we have been back in California for more than a decade, I still get a lump in my throat when we visit because going back still feels like being at home. When we moved to Fergus Falls, not too far from Fargo, North Dakota, some people said it was not the end of the world, but you could almost see it from there. It is a beautiful little city that reminds me of Andy Griffith's hometown of Mayberry. American flags are proudly displayed on picturesque front porches. Just outside the city limits are acres and acres of farmland dotted with lakes as far as the eye can see. Large formations of migratory birds regularly fly overhead, marking the seasons by the direction they are headed. Long colorless months during which everything is frozen signal the beginning of ice fishing and skating on lakes that are solid enough to drive on. Sometimes after a few months of being cooped up inside, I would grudgingly refer to the winter as "Arctic Hell," especially on days when the temperature hung well below zero degrees. When the first crocus popped through the crusty snow and bloomed it was almost like magic—a reminder that spring was really just around the corner.

PREPARING THE SOIL

There were plenty of farms in Otter Tail County. The farmers were always preparing, cultivating, or harvesting the rich soil. Everything had a distinct season. But each season needed to be lived out to the fullest. The farmer who planted not only had to be fully present to stay on task, but also thinking ahead to what would need to be done in the next season. He learned from seasons past what worked and what didn't, but that was not where his eyes were fixed. He stayed fully in the season, whatever that season was, making sure he laid a good groundwork for the next season. It wasn't just a matter of preference; it was a matter of survival.

THE RIGHT TIME

When Amy was only about five years old, we put in a small garden. John carefully tilled the area for our garden, helped to make little rows, and purchased the right seeds for what we wanted to grow. He showed the kids how to plant corn, carrots, and beets and made mounds for the small selection of zucchini and cantaloupe vines.

Every day the kids would go out and carefully sprinkle the seeds with water, making sure any weeds that popped up were removed. We talked about the wonderful, fresh produce and entertained the idea of the recipes we would try when we harvested the fruit of out labor. Soon, tiny bulges began to form where the seed sprouted and pushed through the cultivated dirt. The warm sun continued to coax the little seedlings to life. Little fernlike tops stretched out on the carrot row. The sight of the green plants made the work worth the wait. One day as we watered, Amy decided to check on the progress of the baby carrots. She must have pulled at least two dozen pale little matchstick-sized roots before she announced that they weren't ready. I looked over and gasped. At my reaction, she tried to stick the plants back into the ground, but it was no use.

"You can't replant those," I explained. "If you pick them before they're ready, they stop growing."

Everything has a season. Some seasons just last longer and are more tiring than others. But just like the long Minnesota winters, they will eventually pass.

QUENCHED AND COMFORTED

I opted to teach our kids at home for a few years until they were reading, writing, and understanding the concepts of math before enrolling them in a traditional school. Nathan, our oldest, really struggled with anything and everything that had to do with academics. Emma, who was only fourteen months younger, caught on quickly, which didn't help matters. While I was using flash cards in hope that Nathan would identify his numbers up to twenty, she would chime in that she could count backward from one hundred by twos.

Teaching Nathan to read was hard work that often tried my patience beyond what I thought possible. We worked hard every day on lessons. I wondered if I really could teach my own kids the basics. I wondered if maybe I was doing something wrong. I wondered if the season would ever end, but more importantly—would it be worth it?

One day when Nathan was about seven I stood outside, working on sanding kitchen cabinet doors for repainting. I could feel sweat beads roll between my shoulder blades and dampen my T-shirt as the small hand sander created clouds of talc-fine dust.

The humidity made breathing difficult. I heard the back porch door snap shut, then the distinct clinking of ice cubes.

I looked up into the beaming face of Nathan. He walked toward me, a tall glass of liquid in his outstretched hand.

"It's lemonade," he said. "I made it by myself because you taught me to read."

The worry I had over making a difference melted away more quickly than the ice cubes in my glass. I was doing the right thing in the right season, and I just needed to keep my hand to the plow and continue to move forward until the season changed.

PARENTING IS FULL OF SEASONS

One of the families that we still stay in contact with from our time in Minnesota is Bob and Ginger. Before they had kids, Ginger was a registered nurse in a busy OB/GYN ward. She and Bob married while he was going through his residency to become a family practice doctor. After they brought their son Andrew home from the hospital, Ginger changed her career path and became a stay-at-home mom.

Life with one little boy can be busy. When Michael came along a few years later, keeping up with her active boys became more than a full-time job. She made sure they got to hockey practices and games in the winter and soccer practices and games in the summer. The car was always loaded with sports gear and Gatorade bottles.

Bob and Ginger were thrilled for their oldest son Andrew, but when it was time for him to leave for college, they had bittersweet, mixed feelings. He was so excited about the prospects of his new season, but for Bob and Ginger, it was the closing of a season they had cherished.

"We were just at a loss," said Ginger. "On our way home we decided to re-do the bathroom so we would have something to do to help us keep our mind off of missing Andrew and getting all weepy. So we stopped at a tile shop and the salesman started asking us basic questions like, "What kind and color of tile where you thinking of using? What size is your bathroom?"

"I had no idea," replied Ginger. "We had just dropped our son off at college and we needed a project! I bought wall tile, floor tile, and grout for the bathroom. Once we got home we went right to work ripping out the old bathroom fixtures and tile. Then we rented a tile saw, figured out how to lay in the tile, and grouted it. It was a big job, but it helped get us through it."

Bob and Ginger have always been adventurous, but tackling a whole bathroom remodel is pretty extreme.

"Michael just rolled his eyes and told us not to get all weird on him since he was the only one left at home."

Not only did they still have Michael at home, but they still had a houseful of other teenage boys who played on the same sport teams and went to the same youth group and school. Having a crowd around kept the house alive with energy.

When Michael graduated and moved to the Twin Cities to attend the same college as Andrew, Bob and Ginger decided that instead of remodeling part of the house, they would take the time and go to the family cabin for a week. They recognized the need to spend time with each other. A relaxing transition gave them time to breathe before heading back home where the house was painfully quiet. After years of Lego making, soccer practice, homework, and nighttime reading, the house was empty. The boys were grown and gone.

Ginger didn't go back into the medical field, even though that is what she had been trained for.

"I did pick up a small part-time job, to help put the boys through college," said Ginger. "Each season of life has its own unique purpose. You may be a mom whose life is busy with kids, and when that is over, there is a void because things are different. That doesn't mean life is over. But I am still doing what God created me to do; he still has a plan and a purpose for me in this new season."

Ginger used the free time to become more active in politics and volunteer at hospice. She and Bob had always been involved in their church's youth group, and when their boys left for college, they still stayed on staff, helping with other kids from the community.

"I tell the junior high school kids to give me their schedules, whether it is sports or music-related," Ginger said. "I am not going to be able to make every event, but I will try to come to see at least one thing they are in. I want them to know it isn't because I want to see the game or the performance—I am coming just for them!"

SEASONS CHANGE

There were a lot of things I was in charge of when our kids were young. I planned all the birthday parties down to the cup-cakes. I made Easter outfits. I decorated cookies for class parties, but when it came to loose teeth, that was John's job. I could never handle the sucking sound of a tooth being pulled from a child's gum line. When they wanted to stand underneath me and show me their wiggly tooth, it just gave me the creeps. John was not only the tooth wiggler but also the tooth puller. Sometimes that worked out, sometimes not. Like the time when Jack was holding onto his forearm as if attempting a chin-up. His eyes bugged out as he screamed. Finally John took his fingers out of Jack's mouth and asked what the problem was.

"That is the wrong tooth!" Jack gasped.

John decided to try again later, much later. Usually he would reach his sausage-sized fingers into their small mouths, grab the tooth and give a quick yank. Sometimes he would use a napkin to make sure he could get a good grip on it. The tooth would usually pop right out to the delight of the child who anxiously waited for the tooth fairy to visit.

When Amy lost her first tooth, she tucked the tooth into the small bowl we conveniently kept on the counter so the tooth fairy didn't wake the sleeping children. She exclaimed how her cousins had said the fairy not only left money but also a trail of fairy dust! Fairy dust? We had never done a fairy dust routine with the other kids. How dare my brother not send out an all-points bulletin when he added this important element to the whole tooth fairy scene, especially since it was bedtime and we lived thirty minutes from any store that might carry glitter. I panicked. Amy was so excited about the fairy dust that I feared this type of disappointment could result in years of therapy. After rummaging through assorted craft boxes stored in the attic, I became desperate. I grabbed a thick stack of Christmas cards we had received over the last several years and took off the rubber band. I searched through about a dozen before I found a few with red, gold, and green glitter designs. I took a butter knife and scrapped the glitter onto a sheet of paper, relieved that the tooth fairy image wouldn't be tarnished even if the dust looked like a combination of Christmas and Cinco de Mayo celebrations.

SAY GOOD-BYE TO BABY TEETH

Sue Peppers, a friend and fellow writer, likened the transition of having our kids move out to losing a first tooth.

"At first there is a slight wiggle, and you know that change is around the corner," said Sue, who has two grown sons and a full career in media production. "It is sore, and you know it is going to happen. Then you can twist and turn it. You know it is inevitable and going to come out, so you don't want to touch it. But then, out it comes. There can sometimes be a sharp pain and a bit of blood, but for the most part it is over. You grow a new one, a bigger one that is more permanent, and that is part of growing up."

When change comes we can either accept the next season and look forward to what it may hold or dig our heels in and be resistant, much like the youngster with the tooth just about ready to fall out who doesn't want to open his mouth.

Sometimes we have control over some of our circumstances, but sometimes seasons come with the unexpected.

Sue, the youngest daughter of famed advice columnist Helen Bottel of "Helen Help Us," had just given birth via C-section to their second son when the doctors whisked the newborn from her. Up until his birth, there had been no indication that anything was wrong. At twenty-six years old, Sue had never heard that much about spina bifida, a condition in which the spinal cord isn't closed up all the way. Rumors of paralysis and even brain damage swirled through soft murmurings exchanged between doctors and nurses on duty.

Sue and her husband, Cliff, faced a difficult season that they couldn't have predicted or prepared for, except to trust that God was in control in all things and through all things. As a result of the birth defect, Jared lived confined to a wheelchair, but that didn't deter Sue and Cliff from raising him the same as they were raising his older brother, Aaron. By the time the boys were teens, they were very involved in volunteering and making a difference in their communities.

"We wanted them to realize that the world doesn't revolve around just them," said Sue.

Sue and Cliff wanted their son to know that his disability wasn't something that would hinder him, but rather something that he would need to learn to overcome.

"You have a purpose whether or not you are made with a disability," Sue constantly reminded Jared. "You are not special just to me but to God who created the universe."

Further, Sue comments, "We have failed our kids when we don't let them dream and think of their own ideas. It is important to live fully in the season we are in and be preparing the soil for the season that is ahead. Whatever is planted will grow."

While Sue was busy raising their boys and being part of a successful media production team, Cliff's career in law enforcement continued to advance. Life was great.

"Then at one point I was asked to be interviewed on a show about what it takes to be a 'Super Mom,'" Sue said, laughing. "I had a career, kids, and a business. About one week later I thought I was having a heart attack. I was rushed to the emergency room and the doctors said everything was fine, but I might need to talk to someone about the stress I was under."

Sue made an appointment with a wonderful physiologist who quickly helped Sue recognize her need to identify all the roles she was playing at one time.

"She told me to think of each role as a coat," said Sue. "My role as a mom, wife, daughter, business owner, supervisor, and worker was reduced to the visual of a simple coat that I took off, one by one. Even my role as a Christian was a coat I could take off."

In the end, Sue was reduced to tears as she realized she had nothing left. She was alone. That was the moment her life changed because she realized that she couldn't carry the weight of the other coats if she lacked a foundation of faith.

"It starts with the core of who you are and not just what you do," continued Sue. "Seasons will come and go, but who you are stays the same and it is important to know that when one season ends, it is just the beginning of another season and that we are still not finished growing."

Sue remembers the day Jared drove out the driveway with all of his belongings. It was like another tooth was loose, wiggling and getting ready for a new one to grow in its place.

"I was extremely joyful that he is independent, successful, and happy," Sue recalled. "Both of the boys were independent and moving forward. I stood there with tears spilling down my face. Cliff asked if I was going to be okay. I nodded and told him I was going to open a new business. But that is a whole other story!"

Seasons can bring unexpected change. Understanding that we have a value and a purpose helps us transition from one season to the next, not with fear of the unknown but with anticipation for the adventure that lies ahead.

WORDS OF WISDOM

Parenting is a balancing act.

Taking care of kids is a full-time job. Chasing after toddlers, helping out with school projects, and logging endless carpool miles are just a few of the things we do. There have been times I wished I could temporarily grow an extra set of arms to help juggle everything we were doing.

I have seen both extremes. Some parents are so intent on the season they are in that when their kids leave they try to hang on.

This is like trying to keep the seedling that is ready to be transplanted into a bigger pot in a tiny container. Anyone who has ever had anything to do with plants will tell you that allowing a plant to stay in a container that is too small will cause it to become rootbound. The condition causes the roots to circle around and tangle together, unable to go down deep into the soil unless physically cut apart or torn.

I have also seen some parents so eager for the next season that they jump ahead, like Amy pulling the matchstick carrots instead of waiting until the time was right. It is easy to jump ahead when the excitement over what might be ahead overshadows the routine of everyday living. Life can get so busy and is full of distractions. We have an unrealistic notion that if we miss something important in one season, we can always go back and do it over or make up for lost time. That is not always the case, sometimes leaving us with a harvest of regret.

CHECK-UP

1. What season are you in right now?
2. What are you doing to prepare the soil for the next season? It might be tap dancing, writing a book, learning a foreign language, volunteering, or even going back to school. Think about what you are going to do in your next season and anticipate that you will gain something good in the season ahead for you and your child.

Glittery fairy dust is optional.

There is a time for everything, and a season for every activity under the heavens.

Ecclesiastes 3:1

Reflections

Compare your "season" of life to a season of the year (spring, summer, fall, winter). Why did you choose that season? What does it represent to you? What makes that season unique compared to the other seasons? List three to five things that are describe why that season represents the season you are in right now.

_____

_____

_____

_____

_____

_____

_____

_____

_____

_____

_____

_____

Reflections

3

COLLEGE BOUND

Several years ago my husband, John, was called to a friend's house to have a tree taken down and milled into lumber. The tree stood big and straight, not crowded by other trees and had an abundance of water. It had everything a tree needed for optimal growth.

However, when John, cut down the towering pine he saw that the rings separating the years of growth were thick. What the couple had hoped to turn into valuable building material was useless.

When I asked why the big tree wasn't worth milling he explained that a tree's strength comes from its rings. A tree that has to work hard to compete for sunlight is going to be stronger due to stress. A tree that endures drought or other harsh weather will also have tight rings that show slow growth. The tighter the rings, the stronger the tree. A tree that hasn't been under stress doesn't have the structural strength to be good for anything but cheap firewood.

That word picture often helps me accept the value of stress. When our oldest son prepared to be deployed to Afghanistan, I told my husband, "This is going to be a tight ring year." And it was. When we put our kids in God's hands we need to remember that as much as we love them, he loves them more. Sometimes stress can drive us to our knees, strengthening our growth.

Some of life's greatest role models are not the ones who can bench-press a tractor or run faster than a locomotive. Sometimes they are the ones who have overcome life's obstacles and challenges to reach out to those who would have never heard of them—people like Bethany Hamilton, who at thirteen lost an arm in a shark attack, yet went back to surfing and boldly credited her faith as the source of her strength. Joni Eareckson Tada, whose diving accident when she was seventeen left her a quadriplegic. Her ministry, Joni and Friends, has helped people all over the world with disabilities, and her story has inspired millions.

Consider Corrie ten Boom, a concentration camp survivor, whose father and beloved sister died not because they were Jews but because they had offered hope and refuge to the Jews. Corrie ten Boom lived the remainder of her life as a testimony to the power of Christ's love and forgiveness. Once after Corrie spoke about Christ's love and salvation, a gentleman came forward. She recognized him right away. He was a soldier from Ravensbruck, the concentration camp where Corrie's sister had died. He stretched out his hand to clasp hers and ask for forgiveness. She recalled not being able to move, her blood running cold at the horrors she has faced while under his watch. And yet, with a prayer for the strength to forgive, she stretched out her hand and took his. Forgiveness fully complete is what changes hearts to be more like Christ. And while none of us hopes for tragedy, we marvel at the inspiring lives of those who have had tight ring years in their lives and have become a radical testimony of perseverance and encouragement.

We say we want to be usable, but often we do whatever it takes to avoid stress. And we desire the same for our children. We try to make sure they are happy and successful and do whatever it takes to avoid uncomfortable circumstances. Sometimes we don't take into consideration the cost of making sure we have a sterilized and stress-free environment.

Just like the tree, things can look optimal on the outside: perfect but useless. Because they have been protected from any stress that results in a tight ring year, they lack the strength needed to survive in a big world.

OUTCOME-BASED THINKING
MEETS REALITY CHECK 101

Lisa and Rod Bogart had saved for their son's college fund from the time he was a newborn. Both parents had college degrees and wanted to make sure that their only child had the same educational opportunities they were able to experience.

"We had always told Zach that whatever you want to do and wherever you want to go is fine with us," said Lisa. "We are behind you one hundred percent."

Zach pulled good grades in all of his advanced placement classes and spent Saturdays practicing for the SAT test, which he retook three times to score as high as possible in all of the categories. He also helped tutor other students and enjoyed playing in the band.

"It was reasonable for him to apply for Ivy League schools," continued Lisa, who kept a journal of those years' transitions. "He had his heart set on going to a prestigious school and really polished his essays and interviewing skills."

At one point the Bogarts turned to a professional counselor to help sort out some of the concerns and questions they had about the admissions process. They wanted to make sure they were able to help and not hinder their son and his dreams, but everything seemed stressful.

"Things had changed so much since we were in school," Lisa said. "It was almost like we weren't even speaking the same language. After hearing the counselor and Zach talk about some of the struggles he was facing, it really helped us to understand some of what he was experiencing but not able to express."

For Zach, being on the top of his game wasn't enough to secure a spot into the university of his choice. When the letter of deferment arrived, it devastated him.

"My response was 'Let me bake you some cookies,'" said Lisa. "But this time home-baked cookies were not going to be enough, even if they were his favorite."

When his mom followed him to his room, Zach told her that he really just needed to be by himself for a while to process the disappointment alone. Lisa remembered walking down the hall to the living room, plopping into the couch, and picking up her knitting needles to knit.

"It was the first time I realized that there was absolutely nothing I could do. It was hard to not run in there and try to help or fix it," recounted Lisa. "I realized that we have really done a disservice to these kids by raising them in a world where everyone is a winner. From the time they are old enough to lace up a pair of soccer cleats or other sporting equipment, we have awarded them with trophies or ribbons for just showing up."

The outcome-based thinking of the 1980s that permeated our society and educational systems reinforced the idea that as long as you wanted something and worked hard to get it, you could attain it. But the reality is much different. Thousands of applicants are vying for university admissions every year, and not everyone gets in.

"Things don't always go the way you want in the real world," Lisa continued. "When he didn't get into the school of his choice, it was very painful to watch. Eventually he worked it all out, but we were in for another surprise. I thought that when Zach got the letter and was accepted at another university the whole thing would be behind us, but it wasn't."

The daily strain of having classmates talk about the schools they got into, such as Yale and Harvard, made Zach feel like a failure since he didn't get into his first choice.

"He would hold up pretty well at school," commented Lisa. "When he would come home, he would be drained and tell me he just wanted the rest of his senior year to be over. He was so crushed."

FEAR FACTOR AND PHONE CALLS

Finally the Bogarts were able to go with Zach to Boston, where he would attend college. But now other questions added to the ongoing stress. How would they stay in touch from opposite sides of the continent? What could they do long distance to be supportive? And how would things be different at home?

"We had been a family of three for so long that we needed to talk about how to communicate; would we Skype, email, text, and conference call," Lisa added. "We ended up settling on a call every weekend where Rod asks open-ended questions and we fill each other in on the details of our week, which has worked out fairly well."

The bigger fear for Lisa wasn't that Zach would get into drugs or alcohol but that he wouldn't fit in and find friends.

"I am social and outgoing," stated Lisa, who traveled across the country to promote her book *Knit with Love* after Zach left for college. "My method of going to college was to jump in with both feet. I joined the band, clubs, met people and made friends, but Zach is more like Rod. He is much more reserved and observant. I shouldn't have been surprised when he opted to spend the evening after we got there for parents' orientation weekend with his new books instead of hanging out in the dorm lounge with his new classmates."

In his own time Zach settled in, learning to navigate his way from the campus to the airport. He has become involved with the marching, jazz, and pep bands as well as continuing the rigors of academic studying. Instead of coming home for the summer, he took an opportunity to intern.

"It took a while to adjust," said Lisa. "I would wake up and look at the clock, calculate the time difference, and wonder what he was doing at that time of the day. Plus, we don't always sit at the dining room table to eat anymore since it is just the two of us. Being just the two of us again has been an adjustment as well."

Lisa talked about going out to dinner with friends they hadn't seen for a while and enjoying the evening. With her busy writing schedule and work at the local yarn shop, as well as Rod's job with Pixar Studios, the couple has learned to readjust to life without their son at home.

"There were moments that were really hard, but there have been moments of pride as well," said Lisa. "Sometimes I just think, *wow!* He made it through this, and we are all going to be okay."

They are not only okay but stronger because they have worked through the process.

NOT ALL CHILDREN OR COLLEGES ARE THE SAME

While Lisa and Rod had to navigate the college process with their only child, others have been through the college admissions process several times. Michelle and Bob Ule have four children ranging in ages from twenty to thirty-two and believe that each child and college had its own challenges as well as rewards.

"One of the things we did with all of our kids," stated Michelle, "was to make sure we spent the last two years of high school preparing them to be more responsible for themselves. They were in charge of their own laundry, budgeting, cooking, and doing their own taxes."

While the Ules made sure they taught their children the practical tools they would need, Michelle also noted that it is important to keep in mind that kids are more vulnerable than we sometimes think. The transition from childhood into adulthood is a huge leap, and there can be a lot of uncertainty for both parents and children.

"We were a military family," stated Michelle. "We moved around quite a bit, so I was surprised at how homesick my oldest son became after he left for college. I was thinking that it would be just another move for my kids, but I was wrong."

Two months after their oldest son left for UCLA, Bob was laid off from his job. "We didn't call him for a few days because we didn't want him to worry, but when he found out, he was very put out and felt dismissed," said Michelle. "We had this huge family crisis that we were dealing with at home, and he felt left out of the loop."

Looking back, Michelle said that she had thought they were protecting him from additional stress since there wasn't really anything he could do about the situation and it wasn't going to affect his schooling. However, keeping him informed would have prevented him from feeling alienated.

When the Ules' second and third sons were ready to leave for school, they each chose schools they felt were the best fit for them. The second chose one closer to home since he had friends and didn't have to start over. The third decided that he wanted to go out of state because it was the best fit academically. At the time, Michelle and Bob were concerned over the extra expense, but just as they had done with the previous college-bound children, they stated what they had available to pay for tuition and discussed the real cost of financial debt.

"He was certain that he needed to go to Seattle, and we made sure he knew all of his options," said Michelle. "Sometimes you just have to trust that they are making the best decisions. Now he is working on his PhD in Arizona and knows he was in the right place because of the program he was enrolled in."

When their youngest and only daughter received a sizable scholarship to a reputable Christian college, it seemed obvious that she would attend it. After careful consideration of what she wanted to study, she turned down the offer.

"I really had a hard time with that one," said Michelle, "not only because of the money, but because I felt it would be a safer environment. Trying to manipulate her into following my will wasn't really going to be what was best for her. As a result of being where she felt was a better fit, our daughter did beautifully and really got involved in ways that helped stretch her. I needed to give her the freedom to do what God has called her to do and go where the Lord has planned."

Yet Michelle admits when the last one got closer to leaving, it was harder emotionally.

"I remember going to the back to school night for our daughter's senior year and just sobbing, knowing that after twenty-five years of parenting my job was ending," said Michelle. "When our kids were in high school, we had them take aptitude tests to see where their skills were the strongest, but now I wish we had spent more time talking about their character strengths as well and identifying where their gifts, talents, and strengths were so they would have a more defined sense of who they were before they got to college, instead of having to figure that out after they left."

One of the alarming trends that Michelle noted was the casual approach to college finances. They wanted their children to make an informed decision.

"Sometimes it isn't what kids want to do when they grow up; sometimes it's more about where they want to go," said Michele. "I think it's a very important conversation to have with your kids when they are thinking about school choices."

WHOSE DREAM IS IT ANYWAY?

I read an article in a parenting magazine several years ago about a mom who had dreamt about her daughter going to her alma mater from the time she was an infant. When the daughter didn't get into the school that they had been planning on, the mother took the news hard. She was more devastated than the daughter and wanted to call the school counselor to straighten things out. But the daughter applied somewhere else and was accepted. In the end, it was the right choice for the student because the college that her mom had wanted was really her mom's dream, not the daughter's.

I think it is easy to want something for our children since we think we know what is best, as we believe they should want it too. Several years ago when talking to a friend, she mentioned they had just finished a year of radically changing their family's schedule. After seeing how hectic life had become, they canceled everything that didn't include family activities.

"I hoped that some things could still stay on the weekly calendar, like piano lessons," said Shari. "I had always imagined my daughter sitting poised at a grand piano and performing in a recital."

"Taking her out of piano lessons would really be a setback," the mom concluded. "But we had agreed that eliminating all the extra activities would be best, so reluctantly, I agreed. My daughter, on the other hand, was thrilled. She really didn't care for piano but asked if she could dust off my old guitar I hadn't played in years."

Shari's daughter not only taught herself some chords but often practiced for hours. When the year was over, the family talked about what they wanted to add back to the calendar.

"My daughter asked if she could take guitar lessons instead of piano," said Shari. "And you know what? She really has a talent that I never knew about."

I asked my friend what she would have liked to take when she was a kid. She said she had always wanted tennis lessons. "I loved running around and being outside, but my mom made me take ballet lessons. I am way too tall and was not limber enough for ballet. It was miserable."

Seeing a trend, I asked Sheri if taking ballet was something that her mom made her take because maybe her mom had wanted to take ballet as a girl.

"Yes!" she said. "My mother told me that when she was a girl she wanted to be a ballet dancer and one day she taped washers to the toes of her shoes. She twirled and twirled across the room, leaving deep scratches in the finished oak fl oors. He r mo ther made her take the washers off and scolded her, saying that she never wanted her to dance in the house again."

Do you see a trend? Sometimes we need to accept that the Lord may have a plan for our children that is different from what we want for them. We might want to protect them from stress when what is best is for them to be strengthened by challenges. We might want to hold onto them instead of allowing them to fly on their own. We might want to plan their course instead of letting them live their own dreams.

College is a big step. There are a lot of new aspects to this transition, some that are memorable and some that might end up becoming part of a tight ring year.

WORDS OF WISDOM

Betsey Hayes, a retired recruiter for Texas Christian University, talked about some of the concerns she often hears from par-ents of incoming freshmen. She offers the following advice:

Keep the dialogue open. Parents want to know how their students are doing. It isn't necessary to call every day, but at least keep the communication open. Sometimes this means setting up weekly calls to check in.

Finances are a big issue. Parents aren't just concerned about paying for college but for all the other expenses. It is important for students to understand what their budget is.

If your child will be filling out forms for grants or financial aid, he or she will need to use their parents' tax return information. For those who file on time, that isn't an issue, but for those who file extensions, it could cause problems for your students since they need the information.

Michelle Ule shared how they handled the financial side of doling out college funds. For their freshman year, Michelle paid room and board and gave them a modest amount every month for spending. The second year of college, she put them on a monthly budget, which was deposited into their account on a monthly basis. The third year she gave them what they needed for a full semester. Their senior year she gave them what they were going to need up front and had them handle all of the financial details.

"Because we didn't have excess money, they had to get small on-campus jobs and learn the importance of applying for scholarships and selling back their books," said Michelle. "It really is important to talk about finances with your kids before they start looking into schools because student debt is such a big deal. Kids need to know what they have to work with so they can make the best decisions."

Fitting in and working things out. Make sure students know they can always call home, but parents must allow students to try to work things out before swooping in at the first sign of stress and struggle.

Taking flight. Not long ago a football player from Florida wanted to sign a letter of intent to play for a team in another state.

His mother, not wanting him to move away, went to the high school and took the document before he could sign it. That may sound a bit extreme, but parents can sabotage a child's opportunity to take flight by trying to hold on to them for the wrong reasons.

Worry does not empty tomorrow of its sorrow; it empties today of its strength.

—Corrie ten Boom, *Clippings from My Notebook*

Reflections

If your child is headed off to college, write a letter to him or her. Be vulnerable, telling your child what he or she means to you. Share fun stories from the past that your child may not remember. Include a blessing for your child that he or she can read on the first day of classes. Find a few old pictures from his or her childhood such as first haircut, back to school, learning to ride a bike, and so on, and make a copy with a fun or sentimental caption. Send it along with the letter.

4

MILITARY MINDED

FOLLOWING THEIR DREAMS

Nathan was the only kid in his fourth grade classroom to have a trench coat and a decoder. He loved truth, justice, and the American way: a perfect mix of Columbo and Inspector Gadget.

Several years later we watched the televised images of the World Trade Center twin towers collapsing, marking an end to our country as we knew it. The initial horror left us speechless. When I finally found my voice I asked Nathan, "Okay, FBI man, now what are you thinking?"

I had hoped he would respond that he wanted to change his career path to podiatry and fight foot fungus one toe at a time, but that wasn't what came out of his mouth because that wasn't what was in his heart.

"Mom," he said with resolution. "They need good guys in there."

I knew that he was determined and destined to go into some-thing that required a bulletproof vest and a gun—not every mom's dream, but sometimes that's just the way it is. We raise our children to become independent and to follow their dreams. Sometimes their dreams take them far from our nest.

When Nathan was in high school, we asked others who were in the FBI or other special task force units what they liked and didn't like about their career. We wanted to know how they got there and what they would recommend. There were several routes Nathan could look into, but the one recurring comment seemed to be that if he could get into the Special Operations Marine Corp Unit, he could pretty much go where he wanted to go after his five-year active duty was completed.

John had proudly served in the Marines and knew what Nathan would be experiencing. On the other hand, I had no clue. Sometimes people would mention how they would never allow their son or daughter to go into the military.

My response was, "I can't image not supporting my child to live out his dreams." I don't recall telling Nathan to live his life to the fullest within guidelines of what I would or wouldn't support.

Others would comment on how he would never be the same once he left for boot camp. But in reality we are never the same after we leave for kindergarten. Unless you have a strong appetite for eating thick paste and coloring outside of the lines, change is a good thing. Then there were others who said he would be just as screwed up as they were when they returned and then rant about the lack of government support. I listened before responding, "I just have to ask, were you drafted?" To which they would always reply, "Yes."

"I am so sorry for your pain," I said. "But my son is choosing to go in this direction, and I am choosing to support him in this decision."

I remember when he informed me that the Special Operations Unit required five years of active duty instead of four. I swallowed hard. I knew it was just 365 days longer, but a longer commitment threw me off balance. At that moment, I had a choice to make. I could have his absence be all about me or all about him. I took a deep breath, walked over to him, and told him if it took five years to do what he needed to do, then that was fine by me and my sup-port would be just as strong.

"Thanks, Mom." Nathan put his arm around my shoulders and looked at me. "That means a lot."

I then walked downstairs and slipped unnoticed into my bed-room.

I closed the door and quietly wept into my pillow until the tears stopped flowing. I needed to support him, but at that mo-ment I needed support as well. I knew I needed to get in touch with other moms who had traveled this road that was unfamiliar and scary for me.

When the day came for Nathan to leave, we met my parents and other family members at a small restaurant for lunch, and then we went together to the recruiter's office where the recruit-er waited to take him to where they would be shipping out. John and Mark met him for breakfast the next day, but I decided to stay home. Not because I didn't want to give him one more hug or see his bus roll out of the parking lot as I ran alongside of it, frantically waving a white handkerchief, but because I didn't trust that I could keep my emotions under control. He had a big three months ahead of him. I didn't want him to wonder if his mother ever pulled herself together. In fact, there were many times during that next five years that John would take Nathan to the airport. I would say my good-byes at home so that he could get ready for the next step. It wasn't always an easy choice, but I always felt it was best for him.

IT'S NOT ABOUT YOU

I took up stress knitting because I knew I would need some-thing to focus on besides the fact that he was gone. We wrote letters of encouragement, and I knew that very few letters would be returning because of his schedule. But it wasn't about us. It was about helping him make it to the milestone of boot camp graduation. Three months is a long time. I followed the small booklet we received that described what each week held for him.

The realization that the time really does go by quickly made everything feel more urgent, as if I needed to squeeze in one more bedtime story just in case I turned around and they were all grown and gone. Some days were what I called gray days. They would catch me off guard, like hearing a tire crunching across the gravel driveway and looking up, anticipating that it would be his car, only to remember that he was not at the house anymore. Accidentally getting out too many plates for the dinner table would usually be met with silence from the person I handed them to. As the time got closer for Nathan to report for duty, he began running and pushing himself to excel in other physical training exercises. I remember when John installed a pull-up bar between the rafters in our large attic room that we used for storage. I would hear him grunt his way through pull-ups, trying for just one more that he thought he could do. Nathan had prepared himself for going into the service, but I hadn't.

One particular gray day after he had departed, the house was empty. I had just finished knitting yet another scarf and want-ed to find some tissue to wrap it in as a gift. I walked upstairs to the storage room and found the tote that held curling ribbon, gift bags, and tissue. When I turned to leave I saw something I hadn't noticed before. My throat constricted as a small sob escaped my lips. Nathan's pull-up bar still hung between the rafters, the din-gy tape marked where he gripped with his sweaty hands and determination. Above the bar hung a small American flag. I was not only proud to be an American but proud to be the mom of some-one who wanted to serve his country.

When I wrote for the *Colfax Record* we did a whole series about what Colfax was like during the last one hundred years. I had the task of writing about the battalion stationed in Colfax that guarded the railroad and tunnels, carved through the Sierra Mountains, during the WWII years. Wearing white gloves, I gingerly fingered the yellowing pages of the paper from that time period. The "Mailbag" section was on the front page. It included clips of letters from the local boys, along with photos that the paper had on file. Sometimes there was good news, like someone who was coming home for a short stay, and sometimes news of a local boy missing over enemy lines cast a dark shadow on the hopes of those whose loved ones were overseas.

After I had put away the old papers and was about to leave the curator said, "I think this is something you might be interested in." She handed me an old Macy's shirt box tied with string. I untied the simple twine and carefully lifted the top, revealing the contents. The box was full of letters and Victory mail to and from a young couple, Ralph and Ellen Kummer.

At that time Nathan was in Afghanistan and I didn't know what words would be a comfort to him. I read the penned notes that had traveled across the ocean from Papua New Guinea where Ralph was a pilot to the United States where Ellen took care of their newborn. Talk of going shopping with her sister and new recipes were among the simple everyday items written about along with the endearing and devoted love they had for one another. Simple everyday life. But for a lonely soldier an ocean away, it meant the world. I began to include copies of the local paper in Nathan's care packages. He said one time that my letters often read like a small chapter. I could do very little for him besides sending basic necessities, which were good, but simple words of everyday living were precious.

I also found out that Ellen lived in the next town from us. I checked the box out and arranged to meet her for an interview. She was charming as she pored over the letters that had been boxed up. She seemed to relive those moments when she expectantly waited for the mail to arrive. A smile crossed the soft lines in her face. They weren't just letters; they were a lifeline from her to him, from him to her, sustaining them until they were reunited after the war was over and he came home to her waiting arms.

When the article I wrote about meeting her came out in the weekly paper, I picked up an extra copy and a small bouquet of flowers and we had lunch together. I asked her if it was hard having Ralph gone for so long while she took care of their only child.

"Well" she responded thoughtfully, "it's kind of like childbirth. Once you get past it, you kind of forget about the pain."

The long-awaited homecoming on February 7 finally arrived. As I waited on Victory Field, along with others who held Styrofoam cups of hot coffee under the floodlights, I wondered if Ellen's words were still true. I felt my stomach knot as I looked at all the other parents, siblings, and young families waiting for their sons, brothers, friends, and husbands to arrive safe from their tour in Afghanistan. I wanted Nathan to be home. But I wanted him to be whole, inside and out.

When the bus pulled into the parking lot, weary soldiers emerged, quickly finding those who were waiting to welcome them. Nathan wrapped his arms around his brother Mark, a big smile across his face. One by one he gave everyone a hug. When I grasped onto him I just wanted to count his fingers and toes. He smelled like distant dust of foreign soil and sweat, mixed with freedom. He, like so many military personnel before him, had to readjust to civilian life. He wasn't the same; he was grown up and ready to take the next step in his life, whatever that might be.

Ellen was right; after all the waiting and worrying was over, you kind of forget about the pain.

TAKING A STEP OF INDEPENDENCE

Bill and his wife have two daughters in the military. For someone who had a full career in the California Highway Patrol and other task forces, he knew full well what being in the military involved.

"Every day I put on my bulletproof vest and gun, so I know the risks involved," said Bill. "If you have a kid who loves to fly, you are always going to be worried about the plane crashing, but you know that if something happens, they were doing something they wanted to do. Plus, I never believed that my girls had limits. We encouraged them to set their sights high and reach as far as they could."

Victoria, now twenty-one, has been involved with Civil Air Patrol for years prior to enlisting into the National Guard and is considering a military career. Elizabeth, nineteen, planned to go to college right after high school. She weighed her options for tuition and working. After talking with others, she decided to go into the ROTC program but after one year opted to enlist in the National Guard as well, where she is hoping to get a degree in clinical psychology with a minor in forensic psychology. Her goal is to work with law enforcement agencies, championing the need for more victim assistance.

"Basically, we would have helped her out," said Bill. "Elizabeth wanted to go to college but wanted to do it at her expense and not be a burden on us. She looked into a lot of alternatives, but the military option was the best fit for her."

But things are different when kids go into the military instead of college. Day-to-day contact isn't possible. Sometimes they have their phones on lockdown and can't call home, which in a day and age where people are just a text away takes a bit of getting used to.

"We sent a lot of letters and emails," Bill chuckles thinking about the money they have contributed to the United States Postal Service. "When they can, they get back to us."

The biggest change Bill noticed was that when the girls came home for a visit, they didn't always fit in with the kids they grew up with. Many kids that graduated with his daughters still live at home, can't find a job, or take just a few classes at the local junior college. They are still indecisive about their futures and are stuck in what has now been coined "adultescence."

"It makes your heart happy to see them become independent and reach for their potential," said Bill. "That is really what you raise them to do."

PLANS CHANGE

Glen and Jenni were surprised when their oldest son Phil told them he wanted to join the Marines. Glen, an engineer from Missouri, had just been laid off from his job when Phil was a junior in high school.

"I was worried about how I was going to pay for college," said Glen, who bounced around looking for part-time work until he was able to get another full-time job. "We had been looking into an ROTC program since I knew he was interested in the Army. But the thought that Phil didn't want to go to college at all never really crossed my mind."

One day a Marine recruiter called the house and Phil agreed to meet with him. Glen went along.

After the recruiter talked to Phil about the possibility of joining the Marine Corp, he asked the teenager, on a scale of one to ten, his level of interest in joining the military. Phil responded with a mediocre five but agreed to meet with the recruiter again. This time he went alone and when he got home announced to his parents that he wanted to join the Marine Corp. He told his parents he didn't want to end up like the other guys he knew who had no direction and bombed out of junior college after their freshman year. Phil was only seventeen at the time, so Jenni and Glen agreed to sign for him as part of a delayed entry program.

"We thought it would be good for Phil," continued Glen. "My biggest fear wasn't that he would be deployed to Afghanistan, but that something would happen and he would wash out in boot camp. I just didn't want to have him come home so full of disappointment, because we really didn't have a lot of options. I still didn't have a full-time job, and college had been ruled out."

"We read as much as we could about boot camp," added Jenni. "And there was a book recommended to us by Francis Schaffer and his son based on the letters they exchanged. That was helpful."

By the time Phil was ready to graduate, Glen had started a new job and with the help of Glen's mom, the whole family made the trip from Missouri to Camp Pendleton, California, to watch him graduate.

For many parents, the hardest thing about having a child in the military is not knowing when they will be able to take leave or when the date of their deployment of arrival is. Sometimes parents have to wait until the last minute to book a ticket so their child can be home for Christmas, making it financially difficult to get them home at the last minute.

As much as we think we have a right to know the what, when, and where in regards to our children, we don't once they swear in. That became our new reality and one that Glen and Jenni learned as well. Sometimes we can make plans, but for parents with kids in the military, you have to understand that plans can and often do change.

"Phil was heading to Japan," said Glen. "We weren't sure exactly what time he was leaving or where he would be arriving. I got a text from my friend saying that the huge earthquake had happened. Not knowing was hard. Finally that night Phil called home and told us he was fine."

SUPPORT SYSTEM

During WWII everyone talked about war bonds, the importance of rationing, and rolling bandages for the Red Cross, but times are different now and the sentiment has shifted. While flags are still proudly flown and waved at parades, patriotism on a national level has waned and support is more scarce.

"When I go someplace and see a person wearing a shirt that identifies her as a military mom I have a sudden connection," said Veronica. She and her husband, Tim, have had a mixed reaction to having children in the military.

"It is interesting the reactions people have when they find out we have two of three sons in the Army. They usually ask us, 'Why did you let them go in?'"

The decision for Tim and Veronica wasn't taken lightly. When their middle son, James, wanted to enlist as a high school senior, Veronica was concerned that he wasn't ready.

"I told him to wait a year and go to college before enlisting," stated Veronica. "Then after one year, I encouraged him to stay home for one more year. If he still wanted to go into the Army, I would support him without any question."

The two years that James stayed he lived at home and took classes at the local junior college, but like many students who don't have a specific goal or plan in view, he faltered and dropped many of the classes he had signed up for.

"When he turned twenty," said Veronica, "he told me he still wanted to go in and was ready. I told him 'Good for you!' When we went to his graduation from boot camp, he had changed. He was a gentleman. You could tell he was doing something he was proud of. Supporting him in that decision was the best thing we could have done. Being in the military really helped him define where he wanted to go in his life."

Looking back, Veronica wonders how things would have been different if they had someone to bounce ideas off of and help process some of the emotions that parents struggle with when their child chooses to enter the military. "It was a new adventure for all of us," says Veronica of that time. "We kept waiting because I was afraid he wasn't ready. Maybe it was because I wasn't ready."

Veronica encourages those who are in the same situation to listen to their children, ask questions, and find someone to talk to. "If it is their heart's desire, you need to support them," said Veronica. "As tough as it is, you have to put your fears aside and recognize that it is their choice and be willing to offer your support."

Tim and Veronica's oldest son decided to enlist and apply for candidate school to become an officer during his senior year at Sacramento State. While James stayed in for one enlistment, his brother is still serving as an officer in the Army.

Supporting your adult or almost adult child's decision is important, but so is having the support of others who understand your situation.

WORDS OF WISDOM

When Nathan went into the service, I started attending the monthly Operation Mom meetings. It was an organization that helped deployed military personnel and supported their families. Each month we packed boxes to send overseas, and we also took time at the end of each meeting to talk about where our kids were and what they were doing. There was always a hug and a box of Kleenex handy. I wished I had started attending earlier because when Nathan left, my emotions were so raw I felt self-conscious about crying in front of total strangers (who quickly became friends).

One of the first moms I met was Bobbi Parks, who now works as a local inner agency network coordinator for the California Department of Veteran Affairs. Bobbi knows the difficulty in watching your grown children deploy but also understands the importance of being there for them when they come home.

"It is so important to maintain what feels like normal for them," said Bobbi, who helps returning veterans readjust to civilian life. "Whatever their family looked like needs to be there when they get back. Be there when they deploy and when they come back. Even if you can't all be there, someone needs to be a welcome face when they return."

It is also important to stay in contact, not just when something big happens, but to let your son or daughter know what is going on at home and in the community they just left. Little touches of home remind them that they are being thought of and appreciated.

"I went from writing a letter every day," said Bobbi, "to taking pictures and creating a small photo collage of what our week or month looked like. It was just an 8 x 11 sheet of paper with pictures of people and familiar places like his favorite Mexican restaurant and writing in the margins. That little visual really meant a lot to him."

TAKE ACTION

Find a support group of Operation Moms or Blue Star Moms and get involved. Don't forget to include grandparents and siblings. One of the things you can do is host a packing party at your next gathering, block party, or family reunion. Have everyone bring a few items to add to a flat rate box and also write letters of encouragement. Many times a box is shared with others, so make sure you include plenty of snack items and a few extra toothbrushes.

Reflections

If your child is going into the military, write a prayer of protection and thanksgiving for him or her. If your child is not entering the military, write a prayer of protection and thanksgiving for someone you know that is in the military.

Reflections

Write a note of encouragement to a parent of someone who is going into the military. Let them know you are thinking of them and ask if there is anything specific you can be praying about for them and their loved one who is serving.

5

SIBLINGS MATTER

When our older kids started leaving the nest, I took up what I call "stress knitting" because I recognized that I would have a hard time. I knew I needed the soothing, rhythmic moving of the knitting needles to help calm my nerves. John often called home at lunch and heard the click-click–slide of the needles as I frantically worked thick balls of soft yarn into warm scarves.

"Do you need anything from town?" he'd ask.

"Yarn."

"What kind and color?" he asked as he tried to be sympathetic.

"I don't care," I said as I click-clacked away.

Actually, I really only know how to make one type of scarf because basically I only know one stitch. I don't mind. It is the process rather than the project that heals, and I figured yarn was much cheaper than therapy. Although I planned ahead for what I knew was going to be a tough transition for me when our kids started leaving the nest, I had absolutely no idea that our younger kids would have such a difficult time as well. All of a sudden things were different. The liveliness and laughter in our home became muted and silent, at least for a while.

HOLDING ON TO MEMORIES

Before anyone left the nest, I also told John I wanted to do something special for Mother's Day. I wanted all of us together to ride roller coasters. It was a perfect day with very short lines. We took a fun picture of all of us staged on a surfboard, and the kids tried their hand at the ring toss. Jack won a giant stuffed dolphin, which he named Spot. He took it everywhere, and after a few years the cheaply-made stuffed dolphin needed several repairs and was referred to as "Frankendolphin" due to the stitch marks that zigzagged their way across the flocked material. It wasn't just a toy of misfortune; it was his connection to an important memory.

When we moved five years later, I began to give away several items. Jack made it very clear getting rid of Spot was not an option. I had seriously considered tossing it out because it was so ratty, but for him it was a visual reminder of our day when he remembered how it felt to be the youngest of six kids still living at home.

For Scott, eight at the time his first big brother left, having Nathan move out meant his dreams of doing things with his big brother would likely never happen. When he would watch Nathan and Mark climb into the car with their snowboards tucked under their arms Scott often thought, "Someday when I am a bigger boy, I'll get to go too!" But by then, Mark had left also.

Many times the parents are so involved in the final launching efforts that they overlook the fact that their younger siblings still need as much, if not more, attention than they did before. What we call "transition" they may refer to as a "crisis."

I wish I had thought about this when we were going through it. I think it would have made the transition time easier for all of us.

But first you have to get your own emotions under control before you can help others. If you have ever flown in a commercial aircraft, you sat through the presentations as the flight attendant demonstrated how to put on the seat belt and use your small cushion (barely large enough to house your hind end) as a flotation device. Next was the "what to do if the cabin loses pressure" demo in which the masks ejected from a small overhead bin and the flight attendant explained the importance of securing your own mask before adjusting the mask on the screaming child next to you.

So if we are going to be of any help to our kids, we need to first be able to help ourselves. I can't think of a better way than to start on our knees. When we reassure them that God has a plan for their siblings even when we are apart, then that affirms God has a plan for them as well.

The Chinese characters for the word "crisis" are danger and adventure. Help your younger kids accept that while things feel a little turbulent now, we can still look forward to the adventure that awaits us. Long after the crisis is over, your kids will remember not only the situation but also how you handled it. Buckle up, hold on tight, and keep arms and legs inside the moving vehicle at all times because the ride might get a little crazy!

THE COMFORT OF CLOSENESS

Our Jack was five when Nathan left for boot camp. The following year I enrolled him into the small Christian school near our home. Nathan had come home from a deployment and was getting ready to leave again. The change was too overwhelming for Jack. Right before Christmas break, Jack's teacher took me aside.

"I am very concerned about Jack," she said. "I have never seen a student go backward in his reading before. He has been such a good student, but it is almost like he has forgotten everything he knew. Maybe you should pray about what you want to do and get back to me after the break."

"I think I know what needs to be done," I said as I choked back the tears. *Have I been so selfish in nurturing my own sense of loss that I didn't see his?*

"Let me know what I can do to help," said Mrs. Zorichak. "I'm just afraid that Jack is going to fall too far behind."

"Well," I managed to say, "Nathan is about to be redeployed. How about if I keep Jack home for the rest of the school year? I'll get him caught back up and keep current with his other subjects. Then he will be ready to start second grade next fall."

I saw in a flash the huge responsibility I had taken on, but since I had homeschooled the kids before, I knew I could handle the educational part. I wasn't too sure about the emotional part. I went back into the classroom and started to pull Jack's history, language, science, and spelling books out of the desk. They felt heavy in my arms. "Hey, Jack," I said. "I think we might finish this year at home. We'll do it together."

"Just you and me?" he asked.

"Yep," I replied. "Just you and me."

After Christmas vacation was over, I wondered if he had changed his mind. But when we took Scott and Amy to school, Jack waved to all of his friends from the backseat, glad to have some extra time with me.

As soon as we arrived home, he was ready to start school. We snuggled on the couch and opened the familiar readers we had already gone through. It was six months of adjusting to transition, for him and for me. When the school year started the following fall, he was ready to rejoin his class. The next time Nathan got ready to be redeployed, Jack told me he had that same familiar unsettling feeling in his stomach.

"I was glad to have you come home before, but this time we are going to be okay and do something different. How about when the kids go back to school you stay an extra day at home with mom and we'll bake some cookies to send to Nathan and his troop."

He smiled at me and squeezed my hand. "That sounds fine."

It was a huge transition for our family, but one that we went through together.

HELPING SIBLINGS HANDLE THE STRESS

While kids don't handle stress and grief the same as adults, they do have unique stages that vary depending on their ages.

Their grief consists of three stages: disorganization, transition, and reorganization.

I totally get being disorganized. I am usually the one frantically searching for my car keys or the recipe I just clipped from a magazine and was planning to fix for dinner that night. For a kid, being disorganized means that their world is not the same and they are not happy.

I talked to a mom of four daughters about this sensitive topic of how transition affected her girls. Their oldest is almost five years older than their set of triplets, two identical and one fraternal. Karen Somerville described what happened when their family drove their oldest daughter, Erin, from Michigan to North Carolina to attend college.

"Did you ever have a moment when you had toddlers buckled into their car seats on a trip and everyone is hungry, upset, and crying?" Karen said. "Picture that moment in your car, only we didn't have toddlers—we had with three twelve-year-olds. Obviously, they weren't in car seats anymore, but when we drove away it felt just the same. They were bawling their eyes out. It was so hard for them to leave their sister behind."

Karen and her husband are from the East Coast, so the Somerville family felt like North Carolina was still home. They weren't surprised when their daughter wanted to go to school there, but the drive back to Michigan this time was especially long and sad.

"I figured there would be some tears, but I wasn't expecting the depth of their sorrow," continued Karen. "That really took me by surprise. The following month the triplets turned thirteen, a big milestone. We really didn't do anything special for their birthday besides cake and a few gifts. I just couldn't handle all the emotions, but since it is something that they still bring up occasionally, I know it was very important to them at the time. Looking back I should have planned ahead, but at the moment it was just too overwhelming."

Mary, one of the Somerville triplets, also talked about what it was like to have her older sister leave for college.

"We four sisters made up a lot of words," said Mary, who also attended the University of North Carolina. "We shortened forms of other words or just names for each other, and Erin was a big instigator of that lingo. It was sad to have that constant, funny communication end. I looked up to her as we were growing up. When she left, I didn't have her there to laugh at my jokes, which was sad. She didn't have a cell phone for a while, but we could call each other on the landline or send emails. Talking on the phone is never the same as being together."

For Erin's birthday, the three younger girls made a small dictionary with all the words they had made up, and for another birthday, they collaborated on a birthday video as a fun way to document the times they had together.

"We just wanted to give her something that would make her laugh and let her know we were thinking of her and that we hadn't forgotten her or the jokes we shared," stated Mary.

Liz also chimed in on the topic of siblings. "I absolutely love being a triplet. I can't imagine my life without Mary and Katherine! Having Erin as an older sister was also such a blessing—all three of us looked up to her for guidance and wisdom."

While the girls missed their older sister, they were still very busy and always on the go. Mary's identical twin, Katherine, was born with cerebral palsy and has been confined to a wheelchair her entire life but is quick with a smile and encouragement for others. While Mary and Liz ran track and cross-country together, Katherine made it to every meet, cheering them all the way to the finish line.

"I've always wanted to make Katherine laugh, just like Erin," stated Mary. "I remember after one of her surgeries, when we were about four, she was lying on the couch with casts on both her legs. I ran back and forth pulling a balloon so that it would float behind me. She laughed and laughed. I got tired of running and holding my arms out but didn't want to stop because I didn't want her laughing to end. When we were older we shared a pink room, talking in our secret language or sometimes not even talking at all and just sitting near each other enjoying each other's company. Katherine loves to give hugs and kisses, and I probably missed that the most when I went off to college."

As the saying goes, all good things must come to an end, which includes floating balloons at the end of a child's string and late-night girl talks between sisters.

The next several years flew by and soon Mary and Liz began to apply for colleges. Yet they avoided thinking about the inevitable—having to leave each other and start a life on their own.

"When it came time for Mary and Liz to leave, we geared up for the change," said Karen. "We talked to Katherine about how it might be different but that didn't mean it would be so bad. When the pace of life slowed down, we were able to spend more time with Katherine."

John and Karen make it a point to go out to the movies or dinner and also set aside time for Katherine to Skype with her sisters. They note that even just a few minutes of contact makes the distance seem much more tolerable.

"John and I are so proud of the girls. We raised them to look for opportunities and move forward with it. We never wanted them to feel guilty for leaving, but rather take advantage of all the opportunities that awaited them. As much as you miss your kids when they move, you have to realize that this is a phase of life that they are prepared for. They have unlimited possibilities in the world, and we feel confident that they are ready to find the direction the Lord has for their lives."

The transitional stage is where parents can easily intervene by helping create new memories and focus on the individuality of those children still at home. This is tough because it is about finding a new normal and deciding to move forward.

CLOSE AT HEART

Mary Somerville talked about the adjustment she made when she left for school and what made the difference in helping her readjust.

"When my parents and Liz and Kath drove away after dropping me off at college, I was overwhelmed," said Mary. "I was at a school with sixteen thousand students after being in a high school with seventy students; I was in a town six hundred miles away from home, when I had never been in a different town from my family before, and I was in a place where I didn't know anybody. I had made my decision to go to UNC a few months before, but I hadn't really thought about being separated from my sisters, probably because it would have been too overwhelming."

As her family drove away, all of the realizations of really being alone for the first time washed over her. Mary called her older sister, Erin, who tried to offer words of encouragement. Surrounded by strangers and without family nearby was difficult, and Mary knew it would take time to adjust.

"Liz and Kath and I grew up as a unit," said Mary. "I didn't really know what it was like to be my own person. I loved just being with them. Without them I felt alone and kind of purposeless. After the initial shock, and definitely by the end of freshman year, I was enjoying my time as a college student. I never thought about how important the two of them were to me until we were apart. It has also helped us appreciate each other more. I think our time apart has helped Liz, Kath, and me really develop our own identities and characters and rejoice in our differences."

While the girls still mention not having a big party for their thirteenth birthday, they made up for it when they graduated, inviting everyone in town who was important to them to help celebrate.

"It was beautiful to see everyone together, take a step back, and see how wonderfully God had blessed us through those people," Mary said. "I don't know if I realized the significance of that at the time, but looking back, I'm really glad we did that."

Liz also talked about the close bond between the sisters.

"Growing up we were quite close," stated Liz. "We shared lots of inside jokes and we understood when to leave one another alone, but also when to comfort one another. When applying to colleges, I tried not to think about the fact that I would be separated from my sisters. I always knew it was coming, though, so I believe I was pretty prepared."

Katherine says it feels like a part of her is missing when Mary and Liz are gone. She feels very sad, but she tries not to show it too much. She knew it was going to be hard when they left for college, and she realized she needed to do things to keep herself occupied, such as school and church. Sometimes she had college student friends who would invite her over for movie nights or bowling with the college Best Buddies program. But then they graduated and moved away, so that was hard too. She always looks forward to spring and summer breaks because she knows that everyone will be together again, even if it is just for a short amount of time.

BACK IN THE SADDLE

I spent many summer afternoons horseback riding with my friend, Lori, who lived just down the road from us. She was one of the first friends I made when we moved out of the city. We used to pretend we were barrel racers in the empty fields that stretched between her house and ours. Sometimes we would double up on Lori's horse, Honey, and trot along paths cut through the tall golden grass that brushed against the bottom of our boots. Other times we would hold the reins loose and let Honey break into a full gallop. We would flatten ourselves closer to her massive body, which would glisten with beads of sweat. While we hung on, Honey would stretch her neck forward into the wind it as if at any moment she might take flight.

One of the first lessons you learn when riding a horse, besides to not stand right behind it, is that if you get bucked off, you have to get back on. At least that is what my mom said. I never really knew what that meant until our Blue Bird troop went to the local horse ranch. At the ripe old age of nine, I was an old hand at riding. I picked the biggest horse they had in the lineup: a dark chestnut-colored quarter horse. I could barely stretch my foot high enough to slide it into the stirrup before swinging myself onto a well-worn saddle that creaked once I finally got seated. There were about a dozen girls on the trail that afternoon along with a few leaders and the trail guide. Everything would have been fine, except for the rabbit that startled the horse I was on. He reared up like something out of a Lone Ranger show, bucked a few times, and reared up again. The one thing about a big horse is that the bigger they are, the farther you have to fall, which I did, right on the hard-packed dirt. I caught my breath and dusted off my Sears Tough-Skin jeans. Then, I did what my mom had always said; I climbed back on. I secretly wished I had picked the smaller Appaloosa. My mom use to say that climbing back on the horse let the horse know you were still in charge, but I think the real lesson is in proving to yourself that you can do what it takes to get up, dust yourself off, and move forward.

Sometimes it is in the stumbling and falling that we realize where our greatest strengths lie.

Pray with and for your kids. Pray for strength to stand up when they feel like they have been thrown to the ground. Life will always be changing, and you will have to find a new normal. Sometimes you even have to pick yourself up and dust yourself off.

While the memories of the difficult times might fade with age, the one thing that will remain crystal clear to your younger children is how you handled life when things became difficult.

They are going to want to know that getting back in the saddle is worth the pain of falling off.

WORDS OF WISDOM

1. Make family time a priority. Try to have a set date and time when you want to have family time. Let everyone know so that they don't make other plans. So often when your kids come home, their time is booked solid with activities involving friends. Siblings can often feel left out since they have been missing and looking forward to the family being together again. This doesn't mean being overbearing—just help to remind them they are important to their sibling too and have been missed.

Our house is always open to friends and extended family, but there were a few times I had to set boundaries and set a time when everyone was welcome. Siblings need to make sure they can make memories with each other and those coming home need to catch up on what has been happening as well. This is your moment to hear and see your children spending a meal or an activity together. It is a gift to ponder in your heart after they leave again.

2. See this as a teachable moment. Are you adding to the anxiety of the situation by not dealing with your own fears and grief? This is a teachable moment about learning to let go. It is a lesson for us and a lesson we can help model for our children's sake as well.

3. Make a plan. "If I could go back to the time before we went to college," stated Mary, "I would like to sit down and talk about how things would be different once we parted ways. My parents may have encouraged us to do this before we graduated from high school, but I was either too busy or too scared to stop and think about it. If we had talked and prayed about it together and shared our fears and worries, as well as made plans for when and how we would talk to and visit each other, that first year might have been easier."

4. Take a moment to express thanks. "For the sibling that is leaving, make sure that you sit down with your family and thank them for everything they have done for you," said Liz. "You have definitely made an impact on their lives, and everything is going to change when you are gone. Make sure you reassure them that you will stay in touch and let them know about your life while away. Email and phone calls are more valuable than you know."

The Lord is my strength and my shield; my heart trusts in him, and he helps me.

Psalm 28:7

Reflections

Make a list of things you can do to help your younger children deal with their feelings of loss as their sibling leaves the home. Consider the special things that the siblings enjoyed doing together and think about how you can provide opportunities for your child at home to continue these activities with someone else. Make it a priority to set up a phone call or Skype for the younger siblings to have an opportunity to contact the older ones. For another special activity, take a photo of the siblings together and give them each a copy, perhaps in a frame.

6

PARENTING SOLO

L ife can be hard. When we have someone we can share the joys and shoulder the burdens with, it makes the road a little less bumpy. The Bible talks about the benefit of having someone alongside of you for the journey. But what if you are traveling the parenting road alone?

While I may not be a single person, I have several friends who are facing the challenges of this season without a mate. Talking with them helped me have a better understanding of the unique pain and loss they face.

Maybe you have found yourself single and need to know you are not alone in this walk. Maybe you are married, but your spouse has left the responsibility of parenting to you, or maybe you are unexpectedly widowed. Maybe you are none of the above and more like me—married but thankful to know how to be a better friend to those who are hurting.

Whatever situation you are in, this chapter is meant to be a comfort and also an encouragement.

THE SAME FEELING

I grew up in California, so when we moved to Minnesota we had quite a few new experiences, having people invite us over for "a little lunch" when they really meant coffee and a snack, eating every variety of hot dish known to man, and learning to drive on a glare of ice without the aid of studded tires. The cultural differences were something that I really enjoyed, but the driving part, not so much. I had lived where there was snow and understood the importance of not slamming on your brakes or jerking the wheel in the wrong direction, but driving in Minnesota was like ice skating in a Suburban. I had a few little mishaps while learning how to drive in the ice, but that didn't stop me from venturing out during the long winter months—until the day I rolled John's pickup truck.

The kids and I were taking a Crock-Pot of potato soup to a friend who had just had surgery. We decided to take the truck since the car was snowed in. I drove down the county road and merged onto the interstate. The drive wasn't too bad until I broke out of the wooded area and a strong gust of wind hit the truck, spinning it like a child's top. I held onto the wheel and all I could think of was Newton's law that went something like, "An object in motion remains in motion. . . ." It felt like we were in slow motion as our three kids and I, along with a whole Crock-Pot of piping hot potato soup, made doughnuts down the center of both lanes. I remember the silence as we all waited for something to stop the truck.

Snowdrifts had filled in the ditches on the side of the interstate, a perfect pillow to catch our rolling vehicle. We ended up sideways, facing backward and in a drift so high the windows were nothing but a wall of white. The kids panicked that we couldn't get out; Emma felt like she was going to throw up because she was dangling over me by her seat belt, and I was covered in the thick paste of soup complete with chunks of potatoes, carrots, and celery. First things first—we needed to pray to thank the Lord.

"We are safe," I told them as we hung there. "No one is hurt. We didn't hit anyone, and we were not hit by another vehicle." I thought of all the semitrucks that constantly barrel down the interstate and shuddered.

I led the kids in a short prayer and reassured them that someone had to have seen us and would be there soon to help. And they were. We made it to safety. The truck would spit out dehydrated vegetables every time you turned on the heater for the next year, but even it survived.

The accident didn't stop me from climbing into the driver's seat the next time I needed to go somewhere, until I felt the feeling of the tires slightly slipping on the ice. My stomach seized into a nauseating knot and I began to sweat. "This is silly!" I tried to convince myself, but it didn't work. I dropped the kids off at school and carefully made my way to where John worked.

"Can you drive me home?" I sobbed. I knew I was fine in my head, but my body went into the same flight or fight reaction that I had felt during the accident, only this time it was much more intense. It took a long time to work through and get over. To be totally honest, the fear still bubbles up when I drive through inclement weather; it is a reminder to turn over all my fears to the Lord.

No matter what the storms of life bring, we are never really alone.

FEELINGS OF BEING LEFT

I remember when I heard from my friend Sara, a fellow writer and beautiful sister in the Lord. She had sent me an email and mentioned that her family might be losing their home. She knew we had lost ours, so she had some questions and asked if I could call her.

When she told me that the reason their home was in jeopardy was because her husband of more than twenty-three years had just left her and their two sons, I was at a loss for words. I knew what to say about a house, but I didn't know what to do about the deeper pain she was feeling. It was a devastating blow. There was so much to process. The feelings of betrayal and rejection left her wondering how they would survive. Plus, she was faced with an additional challenge: Sara is legally blind.

"I never saw that as a handicap," she said. "But all of a sudden I felt so vulnerable, and I knew my options were limited. I have a condition that leaves such a small amount of vision. . . . I was raised in a seeing society to be just like everyone else. My husband had abandoned me, and it really changed how I valued and saw myself, even to the point of wondering how God felt about me."

After the divorce papers were signed and agreements made, Sara began to carefully and prayerfully weigh her options: stay where she was until the bank foreclosed on the house while hoping she could bring in enough income to make ends meet or take her parents up on their offer to move in with them until she regained her footing and had time to catch her breath.

"I just think we all need a break from the stress," said Sara, who had to make all the arrangements for boxing up what she wanted to save and what needed to be donated or sold. "We decided to give it a try."

What was a fresh start for Sara and her youngest son Tommy became a closed door with her adult son Benjamin, twenty-three, who decided to stay behind in the city where he had a job and friends.

"I was devastated when Benjamin told me he wanted to stay," recalled Sara. "When my ex-husband left, Benjamin had felt the burden to step up to the plate. He helped make meals and do the grocery shopping as well as run errands for me. He wanted us close but also wanted his independence. He was worried about me, but he was probably even more concerned for his younger brother who had to leave his school and friends. I was very sure he would change his mind, but he didn't."

For Sara, moving away brought with it the harsh reality that her family would never be together again and would never be the same. The hurt was deep, like a raw wound that had been reopened.

"I felt the same deep pain as I did when my husband left and took it as being rejected all over again," Sara recalled while confiding in a friend. "See," I told her. "He left too. I didn't realize what I was saying or really what I was feeling until I talked to a friend about it and she pointed out that what Benjamin is doing is totally different from what his dad had done. He was doing what he is supposed to do. He was taking a step of independence. He was not abandoning anybody; he was just growing up."

Looking back, Sara sees that putting her son's need for natural independence and the abandonment of her husband in the same category was wrong, but at the time, that is how she felt. Their mother/son bond was tighter because they had to cope with the loss and weather the storm of having their family fall apart. But things needed to find a new normal and be able to move forward.

"I was fighting to keep everything familiar and secure but Benjamin really needed the opportunity to grow up and move on, and so did Tommy and I."

A few months later Sara and Tommy relocated to a different state and moved back to her parent's home, where she had grown up. It was an adjustment for all of them, but after the end of the six-month trial period approached the vibrant mom decided to stay longer and admitted that it had given her time to heal her broken heart and spend time with Tommy, who also struggled with the new family dynamics.

"My married friends whose kids have moved out don't understand why the loss was so painful. Only those who have lived through the nightmare of divorce understood. My advice to other single parents it to prepare yourself in advance for the unexpected sense of loss," Sara counseled. "Prepare your heart before kids start leaving and don't communicate your mixed emotions in such a way that they will feel guilty for becoming adults."

IDENTITY CRISIS TIMES TWO

I remember going to a dentist's office and having to fill out the new patient form, especially the small line that asks what your occupation is. I was among those who planned play dates over power lunches, was ecstatic when all the socks made it out of the dryer with their mate, and had a case of "car pool" tunnel syndrome. We have six kids, for heaven's sake! I should have put down that I was a nonprofit day care.

What do you write down when your job and career is packing lunches, reading stories, and being the one to make sure nothing goes into your toddler's mouth, ears, and nose that shouldn't be there, like pencils or pennies? I looked at the blank and wrote "mom," which upside down looks like the word "wow." Then, I crossed it out and scribbled in "domestic goddess."

It is hard to maintain an identity when our lives and priorities are changed. I have been known as someone's mom for decades, and it will be a title I am honored to carry, but being Mom isn't the only thing that I am and making sure I remember that is important as well.

~

For Jan Coleman, the pain of having her daughters leave after raising them alone led to a huge identity crisis.

"When my husband left," said Jan, who later penned the book *After the Locusts: Restoring Ruined Dreams, Reclaiming Wasted Years.* "I lost my identity as a wife. When my daughters left, I lost my identity as a mom. It was a very difficult time because I didn't know who I was as a person. All I had been was a wife and a mom. That was all I wanted to be, but all of a sudden, everything changed."

Being abandoned by their dad sent Jan's two preteen daughters into a tailspin that resulted in years of rebellion. "It was only me dealing with the emotional wreckage for all of us," says Jan.

The biggest burden Jan carried was the sense of loss and knowing that her girls' childhood years could never be replaced.

"The thing that saved me was my strong support of single women friends," said Jan. "It was a sisterhood that supported each other during those times of pain and wondering if you are on the right track as a parent because you're constantly trying to be both mother and father. In my case, I probably bent too much under the burden and didn't hold my ground on some parenting issues I should have. I was trying to compensate for the love and attention they didn't get from their dad after he left."

When it came time for the girls to leave home, Jan struggled with letting go of the loss. She wished things had been more what she had considered "normal." But Jan is quick to let others know that letting go of your past is the best way to move forward.

"I was constantly trying to mother them, and they didn't want that," continued Jan. "What I thought was love and protection they took as being controlling and overbearing. Finally, I went to a counselor who told me, 'Jan, you are still attached by the umbilical cord. You have to cut it.' I didn't see that until she said it, but it was true. I had to cut that life cord that I kept them tethered to me by."

FINDING A CAREER

"When my husband left I was not a career woman. I was a full-time wife and mom and all of a sudden I was not only by myself but I had to support myself," continued Jan.

Thankfully, Jan had always loved writing, and when her second daughter was in kindergarten, she took a writing class that opened up a whole world of opportunities. Soon after going to the local paper to ask about writing articles, she was approached about having a column of her own.

"It was a lot of fun. I learned how to work with deadlines and word counts and conduct interviews," said Jan. "When it became clear I needed to get a job, I applied for a job writing for a senator's office. I was hired because of my writing skills but looking back I see God's provision. I am so thankful to have found something I enjoy doing."

Jan is quick to encourage others that the Lord really does restore the years the locusts have eaten.

Change is part of life. Sometimes we are part of making the choices that result in that change and sometimes we aren't. The best way to move forward is to acknowledge the fact that "normal" is always changing and to establish that our identity is not just in what we have done, but in whose we are; loved and created by the Creator. We have value apart from our spouse and apart from our kids. It is hard to remember that when we feel like things aren't normal or under our control, so take it to prayer and share the burden with those who care.

For both Sara and Jan, their circle of friends became a huge comfort and means of support. Friends they could confide in and pray with became kindred sisters.

If you are single and moving toward the transition of your children leaving, find a friend you can trust to be a comfort and offer sound advice. If you are not single, be willing to be a friend to someone whose burdens may be different from yours, and be sensitive to the fact that they are traveling the parenting road solo.

WORDS OF WISDOM

Sara learned a lot about parenting and about herself after going through the divorce. She shared this:

1. Be prepared for attitude problems and know it is part of the separation process.

2. Resist the temptation to make the battle about you or assume that a young adult should understand what you are going through. Some things they simply won't understand until they have been married or experienced their first major breakup.

3. Don't let fear cause you to put up with disrespect.

4. Let God be your backbone. We may not have the support of a spouse, but we do have God to call on for strength, the right words, or for wisdom to know when to say what is on your heart and in your mind.

For those who have friends in a single parenting situation, be sensitive to their needs during this time and be willing to offer emotional support.

Those who know your name trust in you, for you, LORD, have never forsaken those who seek you.

Psalm 9:10

Like apples of gold in settings of silver is a word spoken in right circumstances.

Proverbs 25:11, NASB

Reflections

If you are a single parent, make a list of resources and activities in your area that can help you make the transition as your child leaves the nest. These might include:

- Becoming a mentor for a local MOPS (Mothers of Preschoolers) group.
- Attending a support group or singles group at a church.
- Starting a book club and studying this book together.

_____

_____

_____

_____

_____

_____

_____

_____

_____

_____

Reflections

7

COPING AS COUPLES

Scientific studies have proven that males and females think and act differently because their brains work with different abilities. An article in the March 10, 2010, *Huffington Post* cited that men tend to focus better than women, but women multitask more efficiently than men. The study also showed that men and women process information, solve problems, and worry different-ly. The 2010 report encouraged men and women to work together on problem solving because they would have a better grasp on the whole picture, since both genders have different sets of strengths.[1]

God made us male and female, each with our own issues that we would need to overcome. And each with our own strengths that would help us be better equipped to help our spouse and our families.

This is something John and I have known for about twenty-eight years and counting. But every once in a while, the difference is more obvious, especially when it comes to clothes.

"Why do you have so many pants?" John asked one day, pointing to the shelves that contained my clothes. He leads a simple wardrobe life.

"I don't," I said as I began to explain what seemed like a no-brainer. "I have three pairs of pants for everyday wear, two for nicer occasions, one pair of overalls for working outside, one pair of jeans for blackberry picking, and another pair for painting."

I looked at the blank look on John's face and continued.

"I have three pair of capris and one pair of gauchos, but they are seasonal so don't actually count. Plus, I keep one pair handy for that chocolate time of the month and family reunion potlucks. Four of the pants on the top shelf I haven't worn for at least a decade and the only way they will ever fit is if I get a tapeworm, but to toss them out would signal weight loss defeat."

Gracefully, I motioned toward the stack like Vanna White right before she turns over a letter and smiled. "So, while it may look like I have an overabundance of pants to you, in reality, I have almost nothing to wear!"

Stunned, John turned to leave then tried again, "Why does one woman need so many pairs of black shoes?" I looked at him in disbelief.

The next weekend we were in the garage. I noticed his open toolbox next to the paint cans. "Why does one person need so many screwdrivers?" I asked.

Skip the Venus and Mars concept. Men are from Home Depot and women are from Target.

We can look at the same exact thing, yet see it as totally different. We now have an agreement: John stays clear of my side of the closet, and I don't mention toolboxes.

CONQUER AND DIVIDE

The previously cited *Huffington Post* study also reported that women tend to be more relational and men more analytical. Our kids had that fact pegged at an early age, which is why when kids needs something fixed, they go to Dad, but if they want to keep the kitten they found at the end of the driveway, they approach Mom.

If they really want a cookie and Mom already said "No," they will try, at least once, to ask Dad before he has a chance to talk to Mom. When Mom sees her little munchkin munching on a treat just moments before dinner is on the table, a big heaping dish of tension is quickly added to the menu. Hopefully, parents have rallied together early on in the parenting years because a cookie-sized issue when their kids are toddlers will usually be something much bigger when they hit their teen and young adult years. Parents need to understand and accept their differences and be united in what is best for their kids, which includes not allowing them to divide and conquer.

I heard about a dad secretly paying for his college son's health club membership because he didn't want him to not be able to enjoy the benefits of going to the gym while going to school. The mom, however, had already said she didn't support that decision. She didn't want their son to have an expectation of a lifestyle that he might not be able to afford. She wanted him to understand that sometimes you have to do without because you can't afford luxury items and help their son learn the importance of living within his means.

The son was obviously pleased with the fact that he had been divisive, since he was still sending his dad the bill. But what about the long-term damage? When the mom finds out, will she be okay with the fact that what she thought was an important life lesson was disregarded? If the dad had really felt strongly about supplying the membership, they could have talked about it and made some compromise. But the breach of trust undermines not just a parent's relationship with his or her child but even more the relationship with each other. When the kids are gone, your spouse is who you have left.

COMMUNICATION IS KEY

Jeanine and Ted Odell of California have raised four children and know the challenges and changes that come from readjusting from a full house to just the two of them at home.

"Couples have to make sure their relationship is strong," said Jeanine. "If they have issues or unresolved problems, they need to communicate and resolve to work it out before the added stress of changing family dynamics."

Ted added, "Couples need to reset their marriage and relationship. It is almost like starting over and being a newly married couple again. Now, instead of checking homework and being in a routine of soccer practice or youth events, couples need to talk about what they are going to do in the evenings and on the weekends. If you wander into this stage of life without thinking and planning ahead, you are in for a whole bunch of changes and some surprises that could have been avoided."

On a weekend getaway Ted and Jeanine talked about what they would really like to do in the empty nest years. Their conversation brought up huge possibilities that led them not only to take a look at their lives but to take a whole new direction as well.

Having married right after college, Ted and Jeanine had achieved what most people think of as the American dream. Ted had a great career with Intel and was on several high-profile projects, while Jeanine stayed busy with four kids and remained active in church activities while volunteering at a variety of organizations. It was busy, but they had a good routine, a nice home in a respected neighborhood, a solid career, and a full social calendar. But Ted says that what he had spent his life doing in the technology industry was losing its appeal.

"The first half of a guy's life is about reaching for success," Ted said. "The second half tends to be searching for significance. I had already reached a high level of success."

When the two of them went away for a weekend alone to celebrate their twenty-fifth anniversary, they decided to not talk about their kids or the things their kids were involved in.

"We looked at the fact that our kids were almost all raised and we had been doing basically the same thing for the first half of our marriage," said Ted. "We wondered what we wanted to do for the second half. When I really thought about it, I decided to end my career in the high-profile technology field and pursue being a teacher."

Ted and Jeanine put their home up for sale when their youngest son was still in high school. Ted put in for an early retirement then applied to get his teaching credential. They moved away from the Bay area toward the Sierra Mountains, where they could be closer to the things they loved doing as a family and as a couple, which included snow skiing and waterskiing.

When Ted went back to school, Jeanine was working, so it was a huge role reversal.

"All of a sudden Ted is at home and can take care of all the things I had been doing, such as making sure the oil is changed on the car, grocery shopping, and other household responsibilities," said Jeanine. "Couples really need to be honestly communicating about their expectations because when everything changes, you have to be able and willing to make some adjustments."

Not everyone has the opportunity to start over with a new career and home, but it is a good time to reflect on what is important. While many husbands are dealing with midlife issues and finding balance, many wives' hormones are on the expressway to the Bermuda Triangle of menopause. Then add to the whole mix teenagers who are stretching their wings, and things may get a little crazy. It is important to remember that you were a team before you had kids. While things may change in your surroundings, you need to hold onto what brought you together in the first place.

A GOOD FOUNDATION

Robert and Nancy Reed have been married thirty-five years and have been through the empty nest twice. Both of their daughters also married men who were in the military. When their girls left the nest, it was a good transition because they had a good foundation early on in their relationship.

"We started talking when Melanie and Emily were young about what it would be like when it was just the two of us again," said Robert. "When parents make no provision for kids leaving home, there is going to be turmoil. We have to prepare our kids to leave, but we also have to prepare ourselves."

Robert made it a priority to talk about how the focus on their home would be different once the focus on the children was gone. He addresses the importance of parents being on the same page, citing that when parents don't make provision for when their children leave the home, problems such as depression and marital strain can be the result.

"This is a time that really starts with prayer," said Robert. "We prayed not only for our girls but also that God would prepare them for the life he has for them. Our job as parents is to model godly living and help them be ready to stand on their own in their own walk. Then, when they leave it is a time of great rejoicing because they really are prepared for the natural progression. We are meant to be a steward of our children, not an owner of them."

Robert says he sees parents fall into the trap of doing everything for their children to the point that they do them a disservice when the time comes to leave. Another part of the issue that couples face is the anxiety of the unknown and having to recognize that their routine will be changing.

"Plus," continued Robert, "there is strength when the parents are working together. Sometimes, there would be things that Nancy would see and I would want to react to, and sometimes it would be the other way around. It is good to have the perspective of the other person and be able to bounce things off of each other."

When the girls left, Robert and Nancy got involved with a ministry called Tres Dias where they now help impact others. It has been a time to make new friends together and take part in a ministry together.

NO REGRETS

For Nancy Reed, making the decision to stay home full time to care for their children meant the sacrifice of having two incomes during the years when she and Robert were just getting their business off the ground. Looking back, being a stay-at-home mom is something that Nancy was glad she was able to do.

"I had a mom tell me when my girls were young," said Nancy, "that kids need their parents just as much in their teenage years as they did in the toddler years. I think that is true. What they need changes and your roles change, but you are still a part of their lives.

Nancy and Robert talked about parenting in such a way that when they looked back they would have no regrets. This couple worked on their relationship with each other, not just as parents but as a couple, which both feel helped model a healthy example to their girls. "My focus and energy was dedicated to raising Melanie and Emily and taking care of things in the home," commented Nancy. "But, we really tried to have a good balance. We made it a point to do the things that were important to us in our marriage."

After Melanie got married and was gone, Nancy says she had a hard time. She was surprised at how much she missed her oldest daughter. Even though she and Robert were happy for their daughter, knowing that things would never be quite the same seemed so abrupt.

Even when there are no regrets, there is often an uncertainty of what to do with the time and energy once used in parenting.

When asked about what she is doing with her extra time, Nancy cheerfully talked about taking upholstery classes. She loves to take something and give it new life.

"When you don't have regrets, you can move forward in a new adventure," stated Nancy. "I think it is important to let your kids dream when they are younger about what they would like to do or places they would like to go. It is healthy to let them dream and encourage them because someday when they are gone, you are going to have to have a few dreams of your own.

GROWING CLOSER

Some couples look forward to spending more time with each other and taking up new hobbies. A friend recently told me that after their son had moved, they went out to dinner with another couple, something they hadn't done in a long time. They realized they were free to make plans that didn't revolve around school nights and car pools.

For couples whose focus has been their children, the empty nest can be a scary time as they wonder if they will really have anything left to talk about after the kids leave. Instead of working on their relationship as a couple, they put all their energy and time into their kids, partly because of their immediate needs, but also because some of the parents' value comes from the children. Instead of looking to our spouse for affirmation, support, and love, we look to our kids to build us up. When children leave, a parent whose identity is in the children often becomes lost as to who he or she really is.

When kids start leaving home, couples need to communicate, reconnect, and continue to grow. It is important to note that while men and women process information differently because of how we are wired, we also might process grief differently. Since this is a big change, be prepared that your spouse may need to talk about the stages of grief and how he or she is feeling. This may be a time when you need to support each other and may even need to seek counsel of another couple or someone you trust. A grieving process is something that is natural but also something that you go through and move past. You are on the same team, so make it a point to not alienate each other emotionally.

WORDS OF WISDOM

When our kids were younger, John played on local baseball teams. I would take the kids along, pack up snacks, and visit with other families. Then when our kids got bigger, we enjoyed other activities. We took several swing dance lessons and loved to practice. Then we had the honor of both being in a twenty-one-piece Glenn Miller tribute band. John played saxophone, and we both sang. We dressed in period clothing and loved going to rehearsals. It became our every-other-week date night. The shows were so much fun, partly because we were in the band, but mostly because it was something we could do together.

Doing something together and learning something new is just as important after the kids start leaving as it was before they ever started arriving. Whether it is going to a free concert in the park, taking a cooking class, or learning how to scuba dive, making new memories with the person you have been married to is very valuable. Your kids are still watching, and someday they will be facing the same things you faced when they left. Set a great example. This season may be ending, but life is far from over.

PUT IT INTO PRACTICE

Take time to make goals that you would like to accomplish as a couple and as individuals.

Think of something you used to do together when you were first dating. Remember to laugh, hold hands, and run through the sprinklers. Have some fun again. Okay, you might not want to run through the sprinklers, but at least hold hands.

What a gift to model a good marriage to our children. I have always known that if the Lord is not first in John's life, chances are strong that I won't be second. Protect and pray with each other and for each other.

⁓

Though one may be overpowered, two can defend themselves.
A cord of three strands is not quickly broken.

Ecclesiastes 4:12

Reflections

If you are married, think about how this time of transition might strain your relationship with your spouse. List your concerns, then talk to your spouse and list his or her concerns. Do you see some areas of overlap, or do you each have unique concerns? Discuss.

8

HOME AGAIN

A good day was when all the dirty clothes were washed, dried, and put away. A great day was when all of the socks made it through the Bermuda Triangle of the spin cycle. At one point, I could single-handedly supply vacation Bible schools across the country with sock puppets. One day John asked me how we ended up with so many single socks. I calmly replied that our washing machine had been randomly eating just one from each pair for years.

"Please," he said, shaking his head side to side. "I doubt that."

"Really?" I questioned. "Why do you think I occasionally find loose change and a few one dollar bills left in the washer? It's my tip."

He knew I had a solid case, turned, and walked away, muttering something about where I thought the lint came from.

Taking care of half a dozen kids is a lot of work, a ton of groceries, and mounds of laundry, but I wouldn't have traded it for anything. While I had no idea when we got married I would bring six additional Seithers into the world, I never regretted motherhood as my first career choice. The house always bustled with activity, filled with laughter and abundant with small things that made me thankful that I got out of bed each day. When our kids started moving out, I felt like a part of me had been ripped out, packed into their suitcase, and whisked out the front door with them. Only a deep homesickness for them remained.

But the great thing about them leaving is the pampering you can bestow on them when they come home, whether for a long weekend or part of the summer. I remember going to Costco and filling the cart with all the ingredients I would need to make Nathan's favorite foods when he returned from an overseas deployment. Sometimes, to my delight, he would give me a short menu list of things he wanted to have me fix for him. Almond bark dipped pretzels were always on the top of Mark's list, and I knew that Emma could eat my poor man stroganoff for every meal. When our older kids moved out, it was amazing how long a gallon of milk lasted. I never minded when I had to stock up because they were all going to be home. It did my mommy heart good to make a fuss over them.

Coming to visit and coming to stay are two different things—totally different.

PLAN "B"

Many parents hope for that special moment when they help their children pick up items they will need in their first apartment or dorm room. Stores are full of coordinating bath accessories, kitchen gadgets, and closet organizers to help with that fresh start. Some parents make the move a big event and see it as a time to make a memory.

One mom I know spent several extra days driving her only child to college. They took in a Broadway musical and traveled along the picturesque California coastline before arriving at the dorm. Curtains were put up and the new books neatly stacked on the small desk before they said their good-byes. As heartbreaking as it was to drive off and leave her there, the moments they shared were precious and marked the beginning of a new chapter in both their lives.

But things don't always play out like a well-scripted Hallmark commercial. Sometimes they leave to the slamming of a door, stomping off into the world with fists clenched. Sometimes there is a moment of relief that the tension is gone, which brings about its own unique regrets.

"When my daughter decided to move out," said Gloria, "she was determined to show me who was in charge. She thought she had a job lined up and didn't want my advice about anything, so she loaded up her car and drove off."

What Gloria's daughter had counted on didn't happen. Her job offer didn't go through. The landlord had to eventually ask her to move out, and she soon found herself sleeping in the parking lot of a hotel in her car because she felt safer there. She didn't want to admit to her mom that she was wrong. During the day she drove to a friend's house and showered, hoping that the company she had hoped would offer her a job would call before her funds totally ran out.

"One day she rear-ended a car," said Gloria. "I was in a conference when I got the panicked phone call to come and get her." Gloria drove the hour and a half to where her daughter was still sobbing, and together they used a bungee cord to hold the bumper on the car while driving it home.

"I tried not to say anything, but I knew it had been a terrifying experience for her," continued Gloria. "She was welcome to come back home, but after she had moved out I downsized from a large town house to a tiny duplex, so all I could offer her was the couch to sleep on. I was a single mom who still had one child at home and was trying to make ends meet."

Having to readjust financially to changing family dynamics is a reality many parents face. For Gloria and many single parents, a child turning eighteen can also mean the end of child support for that child. If that child moves back in, the financial burden needs to be considered and discussed since it is no longer shared by both parents.

Setting ground rules of what was acceptable in her home was something that helped Gloria in tough parenting situations. She admits that you have to start early and be willing to stand your ground.

"Two of my son's friends were killed when they rolled their truck off the side of the road. No one found them until the next morning. I never wanted to go through that kind of pain, so I told my son that if he was ever going to be late or stay with friends, he needed to give me a call."

However one day her teenage son neglected to let his mom know where he was. When a uniformed sheriff's officer stepped into his first period class room and pulled him into the hall, he knew his mom was serious about her house rule of calling home.

"I finally got him a pager since that was before cell phones," said Gloria. "If I hadn't heard from him by a certain time, I would page him. He knew if I put the number 187 (the police code for homicide) after my phone number, I was not happy. He needed to let me know where he was. It is not a matter of rules—it is the principle of respect."

After he graduated, Gloria's son spent a year in Hawaii then returned to live with his mom for a short amount of time. When he left, Gloria downsized again; she offered him the same couch his sister has slept on a few years earlier, which he gladly accepted for a short time before moving out on his own.

"Even though it is a sacrifice, it wasn't stressful," said Gloria, who is thankful that both of her kids are now on their own and doing well. "Even though our relationship changed, some of the boundaries that had been laid when they were younger were still in place."

Accountability is something that grown-ups live with all the time. Young adults often see it as a restriction of their freedom, but it isn't responsible to allow them to come and go as they please without respect for others. For the most part, that is not how the real world operates. You don't just come and go to work when you feel like it and expect to stay employed for very long. Until your children are launched and able to soar on their own, they still need guidance and instruction. The goal isn't just to get them out of the house but to get them onto their feet.

YOU ARE ALWAYS WELCOME

When the oldest child moves out, we move into uncharted territory. We can easily recall bringing him or her home from the hospital, wrapped up in a soft baby blanket. Then a few years later, we help him or her unpack duffle bags after a week at summer camp. But when a child moves back home after being independent, it is a different scenario.

Beth and Jason Myers are the parents of three children, ages twenty, seventeen, and fourteen. They learned a lot when their oldest son moved back home after a year away at school.

While Beth was thrilled to have her son home because she missed him so much, she admits that there were a few mistakes they don't plan to repeat with their younger children.

"I wish we would have sent him to a junior college right after he graduated from high school instead of a private university," said Beth.

Their oldest son's original goal was to major in engineering, and the encouragement from other parents that "smart kids" go straight into a four-year school pushed the Myers toward a decision that became very costly.

"He was our first kid out of the nest so we figured that was best," Beth remarked. "We also were afraid of what might happen if he didn't get into the right school. It could have been a point of pride with us as well. We were wrong."

After dropping one of his classes due to grades the first semester, he decided to change his major. Nine months and $16,000 later, he moved home. The thought of having all of her kids together again was thrilling for Beth, but that excitement began to wear thin when their young adult, who had tasted the air of independence, decided that he didn't have to resume his responsibilities.

"He had this attitude of 'I don't have to do chores anymore; I am an adult who can come and go without checking in,' and it became frustrating," said Beth. "He was more than happy to go through the pantry and eat whatever he wanted, but he acted like clearing his plate was doing everyone else a favor. If we suggested he help around the house, he just rolled his eyes and replied, 'I go to college and have a job.' We didn't know what the proper response was. We weren't sure what was reasonable for us to ask of him."

When their son started classes at the local junior college, his grades began to slip to the point where he needed to drop out of most of his classes, again due to a lack of clear direction. After finishing one class, he decided to change his major again.

"Even if we can afford it," sighed Beth, "it doesn't mean we should pay for something he isn't really taking seriously."

The following semester Beth put her foot firmly down when her son asked if his parents were paying for tuition fees and books.

"I told him that when a class was completed with a 'B' or higher and I was given a receipt, I would reimburse him." Beth wonders what she and Jason could have done differently. "We had been doing everything for him and making his life easy so he wouldn't have to feel stress. I can see how that mind-set backfired. Instead of raising strong kids who are ready to take care of themselves, we have raised a generation of kids with a sense of entitlement."

As for their daughter Heidi, now a senior, watching what her brother has been through has been an eye-opener. "She says she is never moving out!" laughed Beth. "Actually we are looking into a trade school where she can commute from home, which I think will be a positive step for her. Not everyone is cut out to go to college, and students can waste a lot of time and money trying to figure out what they really want to do and what direction they want to take."

Their son recently moved out to live with two roommates. It was something he felt he needed and arranged on his own. If any of the other kids move home, Jason and Beth will definitely have a very clear understanding of boundaries and expectations before they start unpacking their suitcases.

REALISTIC EXPECTATIONS

With the failing economy and rising living expenses, it is easy to see why a little help from family might be the hand up that some young adults need to get back on their feet. But, for some young adults, the hand up can quickly turn to a hand out and the result is resentment.

Dottie Prachard and her husband have three sons, who have all moved back in with them at one point or another. Their oldest son moved back in after he returned from the Marine Corps, another son moved back home after his job was cut until he could get back on his feet, and the third son's stay, which was going to last a few months, has turned into a few years.

"I want to mother them, so it is hard to say 'No,'" said Dottie. "But there comes a time when you realize you just can't do it anymore. We have been living on a tight budget as well. Helping to support our sons has been financially draining."

Part of what Dottie sees in this generation of young adults is the desire for a higher standard of living than they can afford.

"We are barely scraping by ourselves, and we are getting older. It is hard to not take it personally when they don't have the money to contribute to household expenses but turn around and purchase an iPod, a television set, or go to expensive concerts with their friends."

Dottie recognizes that her son is frustrated as well, but the lack of communication makes the living arrangement hard to live with and often feels one-sided.

"We love our boys," said Dottie. "Sometimes I just think they need to grow up!"

COMING HOME AGAIN

Whether it is for a few months or a few years, moving back home is something that is becoming more and more of a reality in our country.

A 2011 study by *Time* magazine revealed that a staggering 85 percent of college grads will move home before they move out on their own. With an estimated $26,000 in college loans and an estimated $10,000 in credit card debt, college students can't afford the additional expenses of rent and other household expenditures.[1] Many unemployed graduates are choosing to pursue higher education in an attempt to wait out the job market, because many of the jobs that open up are quickly snatched up by those with more experience. At first I thought that was an inflated number, but I realized that all three of our older kids moved home for short amounts of time after they graduated or got out of the military. As much as I would love to think it was because they missed us and all the home-cooked meals, it was really a financial issue. Because we weren't able to help out with college expenses, we were glad to help them get readjusted and financially on their feet enough to move out and move forward.

My daughter Emma admitted that just getting through her senior project at Cal Poly and making it through her finals demanded her entire focus. Plus, she had developed some health issues that needed to be dealt with after that stressful time.

"Being home was great because I could finally rest," Emma said. "But after a few months, I really didn't have the motivation to start job hunting in a market where I knew I would probably get a job making minimum wage. . . . It is humbling."

Emma is gifted with the English language. She started correcting cereal boxes from the time she could hold a spoon and loved literary works that most of us don't even understand. She had majored in journalism, with a focus on public relations. But by the time she got out of college, the job market for her field was dead. The industry had changed so much that finding a job in her field of study was as difficult as finding a four-leaf clover on a football field. Plus, since she spent all of her earnings on tuition and books, she needed to generate more money to put toward moving out on her own.

"I will never forget the day I had been sitting around and Dad came home," said Emma. "He said that Starbucks in town was hiring. He told me to get my shoes on and get in the car, so he could drive me down there and I could fill out an application. Looking back I have to say that was probably the *best* thing he could have done. It really made me realize I needed to take charge and make a decision for what I wanted to do beyond getting a degree and move forward with it. I needed to be forced into taking responsibility, and Dad gave me the jolt I needed to take action."

At the time, Emma wasn't so grateful at the thought of becoming a barista, but now she looks back and says that was the best thing that could have happened to her. Since then, after working another job as a teacher's aide, she did get into her field of public relations. She is excelling at her job and able to put all of the educational instruction as well as the life experiences into practice.

WORDS OF WISDOM

In the March 2013 edition of *Ladies' Home Journal*, Linda Perlman Gordon, coauthor of *Mom, Can I Move Back In With You? A Survival Guide for Parents of Twentysomethings*, wrote about members of the boomerang generation who are returning to the nest.[2] She has some great advice for parents whose kids are moving back home.

CREATE FINANCIAL EXPECTATIONS

Help set up a budget for your children so they can start saving. It is expensive to move out when you consider the first month's rent, last month's rent, and deposit. Have them help contribute to the grocery budget if possible. It isn't cheap to keep the refrigerator and cookie jar stocked, let alone the extra utility costs.

CLARIFY THE RULES

Hey, even boxing reiterates the rules before the event begins. Why should we view moving our children back home as any different? Some parents have even written up a contract concerning what is expected. This may seem over the top, but for the parents I interviewed on this topic, most of them wished they had been a bit clearer about what was expected before there were hard feelings on both sides. This includes nonfinancial help as well, such as mowing the lawn, cleaning their living space, and doing their fair share of daily household chores. Think about when they move in with roommates. They will need to understand that they need to pitch in and help. That is part of training.

HELP DEVELOP AN EXIT STRATEGY

Most kids move out within a year of moving home, but having a plan to help them gain employment is a valuable gift. Keep your focus on career goals. Even if they aren't working in their field, make sure to encourage volunteering, learning how to improve their résumé, and actively pursuing all opportunities.

RESIST THE URGE TO BABY

This is a biggie. Especially when they have been gone and you are so happy to have them home again. You need to understand that they are still in the process of growing up. You need to let them fail and suffer the consequences. If parents swoop in and always clean up whatever mess their children make, they will never learn to clean up after themselves. This is true of kids whether they are in preschool or graduate school.

SET UP A SYSTEM

Some parents require rent from their children who move back in. For kids who are struggling to get on their feet and lack the finances, a good option might be to barter for services. I traded home-baked bread for several years for haircuts. It is a viable exchange without actually having money passed between two agreeing parties. There are so many things that can be bartered, such as cooking, cleaning, grocery shopping, and outside maintenance. There are those who may even want to volunteer to have some of the hours transferred to someone in need, such as an elderly neighbor. Have them keep an hourly log so they can take ownership in the arrangement and take it seriously.

This is also a great way to help train and instruct your young adults on how to be resourceful, because someday they might not have you to fall back on.

Reflections

Review the list of tips for setting boundaries when your children return home. Which areas are your strong points? In which areas are you struggling? Write a detailed five-step action plan to address the problem areas you're facing.

Reflections

Make up a contract—something that is binding as long as both parties are in compliance. Have your returning child sign it as well as parents and then make a copy so that each of you has a copy to refer to. If rent or food money is required, then that needs to be in writing. If hours can be worked instead of money paid, then that needs to be clear as well.

9

FEAR FACTOR VS. FAITH FACTOR

SOMETHING TO OVERCOME

My younger sister, Kristi, and I spent part of our summers at my grandparents' house at a lake. One of our favorite things to do was go waterskiing behind my grandmother's boat, the Cherokee II. The lake opened for fishing boats from 8 P.M. to 8 A.M. As soon as the siren echoed off the picturesque lake, it opened for water-skiers and faster boats. I remember being the first one on the glass-like water. I had my feet anchored in the ski boots and the tip of the ski centered between the handles of the tow rope, ready for Grandma to hit the throttle and pull me out of the water. Jumping the boat's wake and seeing how high we could make the spray fly became part of our summer traditions. I would ski until my arms were so tired I could barely climb back into the boat unassisted. It was summer vacation at its finest. But in 1975 everything changed. That year the movie *Jaws* came out.

Kristi and I often dove into the refreshing water off the dock and swam across the cove. Being a little more of a prankster, I would sometimes stop while we were swimming, make eye contact with her, then suddenly make a downward jerk and pop back up to the surface, with eyes widened and mouth opened in an attempt to make a guttural scream. By the time I came up after a second jerk under the water surface Kristi would have swam back to the dock fast enough to be an Olympic contender. But no matter how many times I reminded myself of the fact that we were hundreds of miles from the nearest ocean shore, I would still get a little spooked waiting out in the water on those calm mornings.

I would sometimes hear the familiar theme play in my mind—da-dum . . . da-dum . . . da-dum . . . da-dum—and pull my legs a little closer to my body, just in case.

We can get ourselves worked up into a panicked state if we let our minds run wild, which is why the Bible talks about taking ev-ery thought captive. Being in a state of fear is also part of parent-ing. We worry if there is lead paint in our homes, if we are eating enough organic fruit, and if buying healthy eggs from free-range chickens is beneficial. We worry that our kids might not get into the right preschool and maybe not even finish high school. Every moment can result in a legitimate fear factor.

UNFOUNDED BUT REALISTIC

One day, while living in the rural part of Minnesota, John and I experienced a "fear factor" event that still causes us to shudder just thinking about it. One moment I was doing something and then needed to run upstairs to put something away. I came back into the kitchen and noticed that our three-year-old wasn't there. I couldn't hear her or see her. I asked Scott, who was making a de-sign on the refrigerator with alphabet magnets, where his little sis-ter was. He just shrugged his shoulders, which is about all you can expect from a five-year-old in the middle of something creative. I frantically searched the house calling her name. I couldn't find Amy. We lived near a field and woods, so my husband quickly jumped in his truck and began searching the neighborhood while I continued to look through closets and anywhere else she might be hiding. My worst fear was that she could have choked on some-thing and passed out. It doesn't take much for a parent's adrena-line level to go off the charts. I wondered if I should call 911 and get a rescue party organized while I continued to yell her name with louder intensity as the minute hand on the kitchen clock con-tinued to move.

John arrived back home more panicked than when he left. I craned my head in hope that I would see a small head bouncing around in the cab of the truck as he pulled to a stop. No luck. Our little girl was missing, and we were fearful. He later said the whole time he just replayed all the worst-case scenario news headlines about children being abducted or getting lost in cornfields and not finding them for days. We ran through the house just to make sure we hadn't missed something that would be a clue as to her whereabouts. Then, we heard it, a small crinkling of cellophane wrapper from behind the couch. That little stinker! She, and a handful of candy, had been there the whole time. While we were frantic with fear, she was indulging her sweet tooth, afraid if she gave away her hiding spot she would be in trouble, or worse, she'd have to share.

Our fear was legitimate. Based on all the Amber Alerts you hear about and the news stories you read about, it is hard to not be anxious when our kids are not where we think they should be.

There isn't anything we can contribute to finding a solution if we are fixated on the fear. Fear is a good prompt to turn things over to the Lord, since he is really the one in control.

OVERCOMING FEAR IS A BIG LEAP OF FAITH

I know I am afraid of heights. I don't know what it is about standing on the edge of a precipice that makes beads of sweat pop out on my upper lip, but even just seeing someone up in a tall ladder makes my stomach churn. One day I mentioned to my older son Mark that I probably needed to just face my fear of heights and go skydiving. I put it on my bucket list, way, way down on the bottom where I thought it would stay. A few years later Mark planned for a visit from college. It was right after Mother's Day and he told me he had a surprise for me. Every time I talked to him he asked if I was getting anxious about the surprise gift he had for me. I asked for clues, but he just said I would love it and had to wait. He added that I needed to wear jeans, a sweatshirt, and tennis shoes. That was odd. I wondered if we were going to go cave exploring. I'd often taken the kids when they were younger, and the California caves were a short drive from the airport. When the day arrived, I couldn't wait to pick up Mark to discover whatever he had for me. I drove to the airport and saw him standing at the curb.

"Move over," he said. "I will drive from here." We turned onto the freeway and headed toward the location of the caves we had explored years earlier.

"Oh, cave tour!" I remarked.

"You will have to see!" Mark smiled.

We talked about his classes and work as we drove on. Mark turned off the interstate near a vineyard then doubled back to a small airport and parked in front of a huge hangar with the "skydiving" sign attached to the front.

"Here we are," Mark said, laughing. "You said you wanted to get over your fear of heights, so we are going skydiving together. Right now."

I stammered. "I need more mental prep time!"

"If I told you earlier," he said, "you would have talked yourself out of it."

I took a deep breath. My heart raced. Mark was right. I needed to face and conquer my fear. Slowly I opened the door, and then I noticed the apron I had just made in the backseat. "Can I wear my apron?" I asked, feeling kind of giddy about taking my retro pattern to new heights—literally.

"I don't think they will mind," he said, taking my arm and walking with me to the wide doors.

Forty-five minutes later we had signed release forms, watched a short video, and were strapped into our gear by the person who would be jumping tandem with us. The videographer asked if I had any last thoughts before I jumped. "I should have burned my journals," I responded.

As the plane made its assent to jumping level, I began to feel that familiar fear constricting me. I couldn't breathe. I felt my heart flutter. My mouth went dry. I couldn't imagine that I would be okay to actually jump from an airplane and not cause physical harm to something or someone. Plus I had to jump first. I looked back at Mark, who immediately gave me the thumbs up. When we reached the right altitude the door opened, and we moved toward it. Everything looked so tiny, a patchwork of farmlands dotted with occasional lakes. Then we were out. It wasn't a jump like when you jump from a diving board; it was more like a roll, kind of how I teach kids who are learning to dive off the side of the pool. One moment we were in the plane and the next we were out, free-falling in space. What a thrill to jump, but even more exhilarating was the fact that I actually moved beyond one of my fears. As the parachute opened and we glided toward the grassy pad where we were going to land, all I could think of was "I did it!"

Facing fears head-on can be a scary thing. Life holds a great sea of possibilities, but fear of the unknown can make jumping into a situation uncomfortable. Since we have made comfort and control a top priority for us as well as for our kids, taking that leap can sometimes be a risk we aren't willing to make, even when we have a parachute on.

BEING INTENTIONAL

Judy, a life coach and savvy businesswoman, knew that when her only child left for college it would be difficult. Instead of waiting for the day when parents drop their kids off at their dorm rooms to deal with it, she proactively spent their daughter's senior year thinking about the transformation in their relationship by being thankful for the opportunity to make some special memories along the way.

"I spent time preparing for that transition by consciously becoming aware of letting go in small ways," said Judy. "I had to really focus on my own life as well. Here my husband and I were sending her out into this big dark, scary world. We thought about all those things that could happen. It is a big school; there are a lot of people. She didn't have a car. I am a worst-case scenario person. I felt bad for that and thought of all the bad things that could happen and felt very vulnerable. I processed through a lot of that in advance and realized I had a lot of my own fears that I really needed to deal with. I want her to be able to spread her wings and really be ready to soar."

The thought of sending her daughter into a world filled with the same anxieties and fears that she had when she moved out propelled Judy to take a look at her own fears so she wouldn't project them onto her daughter. When it came time to make the trip from Sacramento to Santa Barbara, Judy took a few extra days and made it a special mother/daughter road trip. They took in a Broadway musical and drove along the California coast, giving them ample time for conversation that marked a new chapter for each of them.

"I had a friend tell me an important piece of advice; if they are old enough and mature enough to get themselves there, they are old enough to be there," said Judy. "The key to good parenting is that if we do it right, we grow up ourselves."

After the first semester, Judy's daughter broke the news to her parents that she really didn't feel like she was in the right college for what she wanted to pursue. She made all the arrangements to transfer to a small college on the East Coast herself but worried that her parents would be disappointed. At first the thought of having her daughter move farther away was disconcerting, but remembering the advice from her friend was helpful.

"Sometimes you have to just back away from your kids and let them move forward on their own," said Judy. "In a world where you can be anything, it is important to help them identify who they are."

Our children must be free to soar without being weighed down by the fears we carry and need to take care of so we can lighten our load as well.

A PRISON BUILT ON FEAR, BITTERNESS, AND ANXIETIES

Sometimes fear does more than just keep us from soaring; it prevents us from really living. There is a tipping point when the "fear factor" becomes more of a "faith factor."

For Jan Eckles, being able to conquer fear with faith has helped her not only live above circumstances that most of us will never face but be an encouragement to countless others as well.

Looking at Jan, the last thing you would guess is that she is totally blind. Her encouraging smile and enthusiasm make her a sought-after inspirational speaker and author, but the petite businesswoman is quick to say that it has been a journey. At thirty-one, when her boys were only three, five, and seven years old, Jan completely lost her sight due to a genetic condition called retinitis pigmentosa. Because of her diminishing eyesight, she had already lost her ability to drive at night, and then she noticed that her sight was getting worse. She became desperate to find a cure in hope of avoiding blindness. One morning she went into her bathroom and turned on the light to get ready for the day. She flipped the switch off and back on thinking that it must be a power outage—then the terror hit her with full force. She had woken up totally blind and began the new reality of living in a dark world.

"The fear factor is really more of a faith factor," said Jan. "Because it is the realization that we are no longer in control. So many times I hear moms talk about worrying if their kids go in the wrong direction, or struggle with the faith they were brought up in. They worry that they might not make wise decisions, which would lead to consequences. It is easy to think that if our kids are out of our sight, then they are out of our control."

When Jan went blind, she couldn't always see her young children like she used to. She had to learn to trust in her hearing. "I had to let go of my grip on the boys and the anxiety of losing my sight and trust the Lord," said Jan. "I would pray daily and learned to trust the Lord to see what I could not. I didn't know if they were walking around with scissors or standing on the table or doing something else that could be dangerous. But I think it honored God that I trusted him with my kids and just admitted, 'Lord, I cannot do this!'"

When Jan and her husband, Gene, went to their boys' athletic games, Gene would give Jan a play-by-play description of the game, and Jan would cheer. With the exception of Jan's blindness, life was fairly good. Then they got the phone call that is a parent's worst nightmare. The attendant at the local emergency room stated that their middle son, eighteen-year-old Joe, had been injured.

"My husband and I rushed to the emergency room, and when we got there the doctors told us our son had been stabbed twenty-three times and didn't make it." Jan reflected, "He had been the captain of the football team, smart, funny, and handsome, and it had happened right in our middle-class neighborhood. It changed my view of life."

Jan talks about how deeply dark everything became, not just physically, but emotionally as well. "There is an unexpected void, and you feel guilty thinking about what we could have done to prevent this from happening," continued Jan. "But, the reality is, there wasn't anything we could have done. In that moment all I could do was cry out to the Lord. *You know my anguish and shattered heart.* It is a daily task to pray for peace and protection for our kids when they are away, but ultimately they belong to the Lord."

No one would have blamed Jan and Gene if they had withdrawn from life and crawled into some hole. Jan talks about the daily commitment to pray together and allow her to receive the comfort only possible from the Lord. She could have been filled with self-pity and anger over life's situations, but Jan is convinced it would have been a disservice to their children, as they are always watching our reactions.

"When we are fearful, worried, and anxious," said Jan, "they learn to be afraid of the world instead of face the world. To dwell on the fear, heartache, and anxiety would have built a prison around my heart that I could never escape from."

HANDING OVER OUR FEAR
OF FALLING AND FAILING

Parents tend to have a lot of fears from the time they find out they are expecting. Am I eating right and taking the right vitamins? Will I be a good parent? Is there lead paint in the house or a recall on our baby crib? Is there an endorsement on the stroller/car seat/high chair combo? We read and study in an attempt to gain a better knowledge of the unknown.

We have seen parents frantic that their child might not make it into the best preschool, be invited to the right birthday parties, or play on the best soccer team. When I was a kid, I used to skate around the block as fast as my little metal wheels would go, very sure that sparks were occasionally flying when I hit top speed. We didn't venture out of the house with elbow pads, wrist guards, knee braces, and helmets with mouth shields. We played hide-and-seek until dark, made mud pies, and ran barefoot through the sprinklers.

Don't get me wrong; I am a big advocate of seat belts, life-jackets, and helmets, but there is a balance. If we are so fearful of the world and what might happen, our kids will be too. I see it every year at the pool where I teach swim lessons. I can usually tell which parents are afraid of the water by the panic in their children's eyes.

Our biggest obstacle isn't in creating a safer and more sterile environment for our children to grow up in; it is about trusting the Lord with our own fears and learning to overcome them.

The other big fear is of failing, because our society has made it clear that if you don't win, you fail. That is not the case. You fail when you don't try. Fostering a fear of failure creates a vacuum often replaced by a spirit of apathy and mediocrity. I can't imagine settling for something that is only worth trying if you are guaranteed a win, much like a carnival game where everyone gets a prize.

We need to teach our kids that success doesn't always happen with chin guards on. Sometimes it takes a few scraped knees to see how fast and how far they really can jump.

WORDS OF WISDOM

What are some of the fears you have for your kids? Are they realistic or unfounded? Take time to think about and talk about them. Do you trust the Lord with your kids, or are you afraid of letting go and losing control?

Reflections

Write down some of the fears you have for yourself, or have had in the past, and see if some of them are similar to the ones you have for your kids. Think about a time when you were afraid to try something because you didn't know what the outcome would be. Did you push yourself forward? If so, what did you learn? If you decided it was too risky to chance, did you regret it later?

10

REDISCOVERING SIGNIFICANCE

Our identity and oftentimes our significance becomes inter-twined with our children when we become parents. Some days it seems like we will never move beyond asking those around us if they need to go potty or need help cutting up their food. The word "significance" means "full of meaning," yet some days feel any-thing but meaningful and more like an endless list of menial tasks that could be completed by a troupe of semi-trained iguanas.

There have been times, when in the trenches of motherhood, the last thing I felt was significant. However, in the bigger pic-ture I was doing the 24/7 calling that I had been given. Which, at times, got a little stinky.

IT ALL COMES OUT IN THE WASH

One of the things I loved about being around my Great Aunt Hazel and Great-grandma Upton were all the sayings that would be part of their everyday conversation. It was a blend of Ozark wisdom and Lake Wobegon philosophy. Anyone who forgot something would pipe up, "Two heads are better than one, even if one is a cab-bage head!" Instead of saying that something was obvious he or she would pipe up, "Well if two and two isn't four." One of my favorite sayings was and still is "It all comes out in the wash." Sometimes, we attach our self-esteem and significance to things that we don't control. Sometimes we allow others who seem to have it all together define whether or not we have significance at all.

The whole Bay was in view when the pilot came over the in-tercom. "We will now be making our final descent into San Fran-cisco. Thank you for joining us and . . ." Splat. Squish. Yuck! I gently shifted my six-month-old baby girl, Amy, on my lap to as-sess the damages.

"This too shall pass," I thought to myself, and it did, right through my corduroy jumper and turtleneck. I glanced up, expecting to see an oxygen mask drop from the overhead bin. After all, the flight attendant doing the preflight demonstration did say, "In the event of an emergency," and as the stinky goop seeped through my layers of clothing, I figured this definitely qualified. My husband, John, grabbed the baby wipes out of the diaper bag and I made my first attempts to scrape the front of my jumper. People five rows back began handing up their vomit bags.

After exiting the plane and navigating the maze of hallways, we finally made it to the baggage claim area. Amy was sound asleep in my arms. John had taken the other four kids to the bathroom. I stood next to a well-dressed woman as we watched the metal conveyor regurgitate various sizes of black luggage in our direction.

"So . . . ," the seasoned traveler said, trying to make small talk in the awkward silence. She glanced in my direction. "Is this a business trip, or are you traveling for pleasure?" She stared at the "Hello Kitty" diaper bag that doubled as my purse.

"Someone must not have handled the airplane food too well," she commented as she lifted a tapestry bag from the steel carousel. I sized up Miss Louis Vuitton and wondered if she could juggle 144 loads of weekly laundry, twenty-four lunches, and four car pools. She sniffed the air with disgust. Gently I shifted Amy to cover my left side. "Mmm, hmm," I agreed, feeling a little out of place and very insignificant.

On every questionnaire and form that is filled out, the occupation of homemaker is right next to social loser. I knew that what I did was important, but I had to admit—it is hard to feel significant with baby goop exploded on the front of you. Thankfully, it all comes out in the wash.

But then that baby girl grows up and begins to stretch her wings. She starts being invited to birthday parties and sleepovers. She wants to grow her bangs out or put low-lights, highlights, and sometimes even neon bright streaks in her hair. She becomes choosey about what she will wear and voices her opinions on your wardrobe as well. Sometimes, I wear my orange suede moccasins just because I know how much it embarrasses my teenage daughter. And if I am really feeling rebellious, I wear the matching orange dress. She'll get over it. Someday, when her daughter complains about the height of her heels or color of her lipstick and she calls me to complain, I will just roll my eyes and sigh, "Whatever."

Our babies grow up and we trade in the diaper bags for gym and ballet bags. There is a rush through adolescence and into the teen years where they begin to teeter on the edge of the nest and wonder if they have what it takes to get airborne. There has been so much time and effort in making sure the nest is cozy. And even though things are getting a little crowded, a mother bird is kept busy by the constant need to find more worms or bugs to feed her little hatchlings. All of a sudden, the nest is empty. The birds have gone, and what had been a constant blur of activity is now nothing more than a few discarded feathers. Silence mutes all that was colorful, and it is time to reestablish our significant place in an ever-changing world.

Hearing those words and living them out are two different things. It is important to remember that our significance isn't in whose parent we are but ultimately in whose child we are. It is sometimes even harder to understand our significance when our main job of parenting is over and we are surrounded by an unfamiliar silence.

LIVING APART

Debra and Karl were very busy with four active kids. Karl worked in law enforcement, and his schedule was demanding and varied. Debra taught piano lessons and was very involved in church ministries, but raising their kids was her first priority.

"I wasn't prepared for it to end so abruptly," Debra said of having all four of their children move out within two years. Karl and Debra's children were spaced out every two years, which meant that when someone was graduating from high school, someone was also graduating from junior college. Their oldest daughter had completed two years at the local junior college and was moving away from home to finish her four-year degree and their second child was graduating from high school and going right into a four-year college.

"They both moved the same exact weekend," recalled Debra. "Karl went with Wendy to Santa Clarita, and I drove Scott to Chico, where he moved in with my parents for the first few years."

For Karl, the long drive with his daughter was a good time to visit and say things that need to be talked over before a child moves out. For Deb, the short drive was followed by a quick hug and a kiss.

"We didn't have each other to cling to," recalled Debra. "I wasn't really prepared to say good-bye and drive home alone."

Two years later, Debra and Karl had their other two children move out. In April, their daughter, Lisa, got married and moved away, and a few months later their youngest child, Thomas, graduated from high school and moved to San Luis Obispo to attend Cal Polytechnic State University.

"It was such a happy time because there were so many milestones, and we were super busy getting ready for each big event, but all of a sudden, 'Wham!' No one was home anymore. The house was so quiet you could hear the ticking of the living room clock echo throughout the home we had raised all four of our children in," recalled Debra.

"I remember driving with Thomas to do errands right before we moved him to school. We rode in silence on our mom-and-son outing. I felt like I needed to make sure there wasn't anything he needed to talk about or questions he had before leaving us. I asked him what he was thinking about and what was on his mind."

Thomas looked over at his mom and said, "I am just thinking about all the robots I am going to build."

Debra smiled and nodded. Thomas was thinking about how excited he was for his future, while she was struggling to hold onto the present. Parents sometimes worry and even fabricate problems, but more often than not, their kids are anxious to move out and discover their full potential.

Letting go of her youngest was more difficult than Debra thought it would be. "I cried and cried," she said, smiling as she looked back on that time. "I just didn't know if he could really survive without me. I knew what his favorite foods were and how he like them cooked! I wondered if he would make friend and be able to handle the things I had always helped him with. Finally I relied on what I knew about Thomas's character and realized he was going to be fine. I was the one who wasn't handling things well."

Debra, who now loves being a grandma, looks back on those years when the transitions were the toughest. She had been a stay-at-home mom all those years and suddenly it was over.

"If there was anything I did right," said Debra, "I knew it was because of my relationship with the Lord. I was feeling lost in my role as a wife and mom. Since my role changed drastically, the Lord kept me centered."

CHANGE ISN'T ALWAYS EASY

It is important to note that change can be difficult. When our kids leave, not only do we miss them, but we also miss the friends that used to come over. Mark, our third child, was very involved in football and in the community. We often had extra boys at the house for dinner, to crash on the couch, and to hang out. Several of them had their own toothbrushes in the bathroom drawer. They were part of our family. But when Mark graduated, many of them moved away as well, and those who stayed found jobs. The toothbrush drawer no longer held spares, and we didn't always see the circle of friends we used to sit next to at Friday night football games. It was amazing how much of our social lives revolved around our kids.

It was a change for everyone. With change can come grief. Grief is natural, and sometimes it even involves crying. But as my great-grandma used to say, "Nothing beats a good cry to get whatever ails you out of your system."

When I did a project on loss, I realized that the church doesn't really talk about what to do when we grieve. I didn't know how to work things out of my system, so I usually shoved feelings to the bottom of my emotion tank until they were ready to explode under the slightest amount of pressure. So many scriptures talk about being happy, joyful, and filled with thanksgiving. There are verses about taking every thought captive and not being anxious. Talking about how to handle crisis isn't something I ever heard in a Sunday school flannel board talk, yet sorrow is part of how we are hardwired.

We need to address how to handle those emotions that often come with the change and transition when the last child leaves the nest.

GRIEF IS A NATURAL PART OF CHANGE

A friend told me once that the only thing we can count on in life is change. Any change can bring about a sense of loss. Grieving is a part of the healing process that helps people move past the pain they are carrying around.

In a section about the stages of grief, Memorial Hospital's website notes the following: "Denying the feelings and failing to work through all five stages of grief is harder on the body and mind that going through them."[1] And my great-grandmother thought that lack of bran and prunes was hard on the body!

Trying to suppress negative emotions by always looking on the bright side sometimes compounds the problem.

When I talked to Linda, a high school friend who has a master's degree in psychology, she mentioned that each loss has its own grief. Sometimes it takes longer for people to process through the cycles, but each phase is important.

THE STAGES OF GRIEF

1. Denial and Isolation
2. Anger
3. Bargaining
4. Depression
5. Acceptance

Denial and Isolation

"Denial and Isolation" is the stage in which you are denying that the loss has or is taking place. You don't want to think or talk about the fact that your child is about to leave the nest and move on with life without you. Pushing the inevitable from your thoughts will result in being reactive instead of proactive as you deal with your empty nest.

Anger

Anger is usually a secondary emotion that follows disappointment. It is easy to be angry at a situation or a person for the pain, even when nothing could have stopped the situation from happening.

I see this happen when kids move out under unfavorable circumstances. There are so many emotions and things going on during big life transitions. Sometimes things get overheated and left unresolved, leaving everyone wondering what to say about the proverbial elephant in the room. It is better to confront the issues and deal with them because they aren't going to take care of themselves. Rather, the issues become the lump under the rug that people step around.

Bargaining/Depression

Bargaining is when a grieving person tries to make a deal with God.

Depression is when the person feels numb instead of being angry or sad. There is a void that is often medicated in one form or another as a form of coping.

In a study cited in the November 2012 San Francisco Chronicle, researchers compared data from 1988-94 with data from 2005-8 and found that the rate of antidepressant use had increased nearly 400 percent. The study stated that one in every eleven Americans is taking a prescription for depression, making antidepressants the most common drug being prescribed for Americans between the ages of eighteen and forty-four.[2]

On a trip with a group of gals a few years ago, I found out I was one of the only ones who was not on some form of antidepressant. The biggest question they had for me was, "How do you cope?"

I thought back to the generations where neighbors knew each other and women met together to learn basics of canning and sewing. They also supported each other during transitional times.

The sense of community was strong because we weren't flooded by artificial socializing. One real friend is much better than a hundred virtual friends. We can be connected via the worldwide web, yet our level of loneliness is rising.

When our kids leave home and our routine becomes very different, it is important to expand yourself outside of the box and make new friends, pursue new interests, and reconnect with people who care about you. Seek out someone you trust and talk. Who knows, maybe that person is looking for one really good friend as well.

Acceptance

Acceptance is letting go of the negative emotions and acknowledging the situation. It is the moment you decide to stop hanging on to the past and start moving forward. It is when you look forward to not only what the Lord has for your child's life but what he has for yours as well. It is a celebration that you have done your task of parenting to the best of your ability and are ready for a new adventure.

Not everyone grieves at the same rate. If at any time along this transitional journey you need to talk it out with a friend, a pastor, a priest, or a counselor, then do it. When you learn how to cope with the change, you will be able to regain your footing and be able to encourage others going through the same things.

SOME FRIENDS WHO HAVE
BEEN THROUGH THIS CHIME IN

Since, at the writing of this book, I have three children out of the nest and three to go, I feel like I am benefiting a lot from this chapter. Since this is totally uncharted territory for me, I asked others how they handled the empty nest and got some great responses.

Jeanette Atwood was one who had great insight on dealing with the sound of silence.

"Just about the time my last one left, the grandbabies started coming from the first one to leave. So the nesting started over, just in a different way. My personal coping skills came from having established a 'more than a mom' identity early on. I'm not saying being a mom is not worthy, wonderful, and important. It *is*! But knowing the day would come when I wasn't in that daily role, I prepared. And frankly, the sound of silence, again, for me, was the sweet sound of success. My offspring had roots and wings and could manage, for the most part, on their own. Sure, we got and still get a few of those 'emergency' phone calls: 'Mom, how do you bake a potato? Mom, I locked my keys in the car.' My daughter was two thousand miles away and there wasn't anything we could do to help her physically, but it was nice to be needed and know she still counts on us for moral support."

Another dad, Pete, explained that when his two children graduated from college he and his wife drafted up a "Declaration of Independence."

"It stated that we would always love and support them, but that our part of parenting was finished. They were independent to make their own choices and provide for their own needs."

Pete said it was liberating not only for his son and daughter but also for him and his wife because it acknowledged that they were ready to move into a new season of their lives.

Michelle Ule commented on the value of spending time with her husband and creating new memories. "We dropped our youngest off at college, and then I joined my husband on a business trip to Washington, D.C., where we saw old friends and acted like the carefree adults we were. My advice to those about to send off their last or only child is to take a short trip together and enjoy your fellow survivor!"

Another friend said that when her mom was struggling with her leaving, she gently reminded her that "she had a life before me, and she will still have a full life after I am gone."

Bev, a mom of four, talked candidly about the reality of readjusting to life without kids

"With the departure of each child, whether to college or relocation, there was a loss. A loss of what was, a loss of being needed like I was before, and the loss of the tie that kept us informed of their whereabouts. Tearful good-byes with mixed excitement and sadness were followed by stages of grieving. I experienced so many emotions at once—guilt over things I wish I would have done, reflection, and loneliness. Then I finally accepted the changes and discovered my new identity and interests separate from my children."

After several years, Bev developed an appreciation for the empty nest. After years of homeschooling and working, she had the time and energy to pursue other skills and passions.

ANXIETY OVER THE UNKNOWN

Susan admits to having a hard time her daughter's senior year. Tears and an overwhelming sense of melancholy would wash over her every time she thought about having her two children move away. Her son, who had graduated and was attending the local junior college, was transferring to a four-year university, and her daughter was leaving as well, after being offered an athletic schol-arship. Both kids would be leaving home within just a few weeks of each other. The thought of how much she and her husband would miss them kept cycling through her mind and heart.

"I knew they would be able to stand on their own because we had been giving them more and more responsibility, but the house was going to be so empty without them," said Susan. "It was hard dropping them off at school. A week after they were both gone, I realized it was really nice. I think it was the unknown that had me so upset, because you think you are going to be missing them all the time, but eventually you settle into a new routine. If someone would have told me that I would enjoy having some space to myself, I would have thought they were kidding. But it is true. We did the best job we could and raised our children to be adults."

Susan mentioned that she doesn't worry about her kids as much as she used to when they were home. "When they come back, it is nice and we have a great time. I actually think they missed the family pet at first more than they missed their dad and me. I will always miss them, but this is a new start for us as well. Things change and it might not always be the same, but that doesn't mean you are out of their lives."

Our children may have flown the nest, but the memories we made while they were there are ours to keep.

TAKE ACTION

Think of a friend you have known for a long time or one you recently met that you can have coffee or tea with and talk over some of your concerns.

List three of your biggest worries or anxieties concerning being an empty nester.

Think of someone who has already experienced the empty nest. Ask how their children leaving changed their schedule.

What three things would you do if you had more time and energy?

Remember that your significance isn't tied to being able to pack lunches faster than a speeding bullet or jump loads of laundry in a single bound. We are created in God's image and designed with a plan and purpose both before and after we have raised children.

Are not two sparrows sold for a penny? Yet not one of them will fall to the ground outside your Father's care. And even the very hairs of your head are all numbered. So don't be afraid; you are worth more than many sparrows.

Matthew 10:29-31

Reflections

- List three of your biggest worries or anxieties concerning being an empty nester.
- What three things would you do if you had more time and energy?
- List five things that bring meaning to your life. Under each item, describe why it is meaningful to you.

Just when the caterpillar thought
the World was over...
it became a butterfly.

11

TENSION, TEACHABLE MOMENTS, AND TRANSITION

One of the things that caught me off guard after we had kids was the fact that they were not like me. I was fairly compliant growing up and would rather do whatever was needed to keep the peace than have tension or conflict. So when my kids would defiantly edge their toe across the lines I had drawn, I took it personally. One day, John came home from work, and I was totally at the end of whatever young moms get to the end of. I exclaimed that I had asked them three times to do something and even said *please!* Still, the result was disobedience. John, having combat Marine training, explained the objectives of taking over hostile territory and the impracticality of negotiating with a three-year-old and an eighteen-month-old.

"Stand your ground," he said, "because they are keeping score."

Now that was a scary thought, especially since I had the feeling that I was already losing.

"But I am outnumbered," I sighed in resignation.

"You outrank them," he added. "Plus, you are the mom. You can do this."

It helped me to realize that tension is part of training. In fact, tension can even be a good thing because of what happens as a result of healthy, natural tension.

Take sewing for instance. Without tension you would never be able to hold a seam. Too lose and the top thread gaps and doesn't hold what you are sewing together. Too tight and the thread gets bunched up, allowing the fabric to pucker at the seam. Not a pretty sight! No tension at all and the top thread has nothing to bind to and doesn't have the ability to move forward.

Even in writing, it is tension that moves the story. Where would *Star Wars* be if everything in the galaxy were one big happy family reunion? Where would *You've Got Mail* be if the characters had fallen in love in the first scene? The tension is dramatized, but it resonates because it is part of how the world really works.

Why should we be surprised when it happens in our home? Don't try to pretend it isn't there and weave a few fig leaves together to cover it up. Identify it, deal with it, and learn from it. The best place to start is to pray about it. There is nothing new under the sun. God knows that we can use all the help we can get when it comes to raising our kids to adulthood, and sometimes we need to learn a few things as well.

UNEXPECTED STORM

"You don't understand anything, Mom. Matt is still my best friend!" Nathan, who was in seventh grade at the time, stomped down the hall to his bedroom, anger resonating in his thirteen-year-old voice. I helplessly sank into the dining room chair and wondered what to do next. From the moment I felt the first movement in my womb, I loved Nathan, our firstborn. Tenderness that had been shared between us was quickly being replaced with tension, and I didn't know what to do.

Please God, I silently begged. *Help me show him how much I love him.*

I had heard how hard going through the adolescent years were on teenagers, but I never imagined how hard it was on the mothers. Until now.

Although his friend Matt was one year older than Nathan, the boys had been friends since they were young. They enjoyed sleepovers, jumping on trampolines, and riding dirt bikes. Anything they enjoyed doing was much more fun if they could do it together. It was hard for Nathan to watch his friend go on to junior high ahead of him. Then, when school started, Matt quickly made new friends. Unfortunately, they were the wrong ones. And Nathan would not accept that his friend had changed.

As Nathan's thirteenth birthday approached, we decided he was ready for the responsibilities of taking care of his own dog. John found the perfect one—a Newfoundland Lab puppy. Missy was just a wiggly ball of black fur when we gave her to Nathan. The two became inseparable. The more time he spent taking care of Missy and training her, the less he was spending with Matt. Yet the tension that had built up between me and our oldest son remained. I did the only thing I could. I kept praying for an opportunity to show him how much I loved him.

Before we knew it, a year had passed. Missy was not only grown, but before we could take her into the vet to get spayed, she became pregnant with pups of her own. Nestled under a faded blue 1960 Ford truck parked in the grass behind the workshop, Missy gave birth to four puppies. Nathan was in "boy heaven."

The next day, we moved Missy and her puppies into the blanket-lined doghouse. We could see the dog run from the kitchen window. It was a familiar sight to look out and see Nathan's pant legs poking out of the front of the doghouse. He spent every spare minute enjoying the lively puppies as they licked his face or pulled on his shoelaces. I was so happy Nathan had something positive to focus on.

"They are so cute!" Nathan whispered to me as I handed him a fresh-baked oatmeal cookie. A sleeping puppy was curled up in his lap and another snuggled in his arms. "I just can't keep my eyes off of them."

"I know," I responded. "That is how I felt about you from the day you were born."

Nathan shifted the sleeping puppy in his arm and pretended to not hear my comment.

Help me have patience, Lord. I tried to smile in spite of the hurt I felt.

A few days later, we awoke to unexpected rain beating down from a cold, dark sky. I pulled on my bathrobe and poured myself a cup of hot coffee. Nathan bound up the stairs into the kitchen. He was dressed and anxious to check on Missy and her little brood. Quickly he disappeared into the darkness with just a beam from his flashlight to lighten the path. Within minutes, the door burst open. Amid the cold flurry of wind, Nathan stumbled back through the doorway.

Panic filled his eyes and his lips quivered more with fear than cold. In his outstretched hands he held a black mound of matted fur.

"Mom! The puppy! He was out of the doghouse!" Nathan said.

I set my cup of coffee down on the counter and rubbed my hand over the cold, lifeless form.

"I heard a soft whimper and found him blown to the back of the dog run all by himself. Help me!" Nathan pleaded. Tears blurred his vision. "What should we do?"

After a deep breath and a quick prayer, I plunged into action. The little puppy was stiff from the cold wind and soaked all the way to his skin. There were times I wasn't sure if he was breathing. I carefully lifted the puppy from my son's hands.

"Get a hot pack and a towel," I instructed Nathan. "Then bring Missy and the other puppies in here. This little guy needs something warm to eat."

Nathan quickly disappeared after he brought the things I had asked for. Soon, Nathan had the rest of his beloved canine family in the house. Missy was patient as we held the puppy up to her, but the puppy was too weak to nurse. Warm milk trickled from the corner of his mouth.

While it was a miracle that Nathan had found the puppy, it may have been too late. The puppy's fragile life precariously hung in the balance. All we could do was wait. But at least it was something we were doing together.

"Missy!" Nathan choked out, breaking the silence. "What kind of a mother are you to let your puppy outside in the rain? How could you be so careless? He might die!"

Gently, I looked at my son, who was beginning to turn the corner of childhood into becoming a young man. I stood up and put my hand on his shoulder. He turned toward me and leaned into my comfort.

"You are right," I gingerly continued. "What kind of a mom lets her babies wander out of the house before they are ready to handle the storms?"

Tears spilled onto the front of my bathrobe; we were no longer talking about dogs and windblown puppies.

"Now you know how I feel about you."

And he did.

Within a few hours the puppy started holding his own, but the true blessing was seeing how an unexpected storm became the perfect teachable moment for both of us.

If I could go back to when my kids were small, I would pray more for teachable moments. Thank heaven; it is never too late to start looking for those nuggets of truth during times of tension.

TRANSITION YEARS

One of the things I loved about writing for a small-town paper was getting to meet all sorts of interesting people. One person who became a dear friend was the Nigerian-born Catholic priest who had come to town. In the interview, I asked him about his life. He responded with this statement, "The only thing certain in life is that there will always be change." How true that is!

The transitional years can be difficult, because it is new territory for everyone.

The year Randy's only child left for college, he decided to relocate as well. "I knew I couldn't stay in my current situation and decided to move from California to Arizona," said Randy. "We stay connected through phone calls and Facebook, but I knew she was ready to be independent and moving into a safe place, so that helped me to feel like it was a positive move for both of us."

Keeping in touch and keeping the lines of communication open is key to maintaining a relationship between parents and their adult children.

"I feel like I brought her up to think for herself and tried to give her a lot of commonsense knowledge without overshadowing her, so she could learn to make decisions," said Randy. "Plus, I took her to church where she had a solid foundation at an early age."

Being able to pray for each other and with each other is an important part of moving through transitions that face parents and their almost-grown children.

TRANSFER OF RESPONSIBILITY

Several Sundays ago, the worship leader, George, was talking about the truths found in Psalm 139 and the fact that no matter where we go, we are not out of the reach or sight of the Lord. George is from Scotland, and he talked about the notion that as the time drew near for him to come to the United States to go to school, he was sure his mother would be devastated. As a small token of his love for his Mum, he painted a watercolor picture of the world. Where Scotland was he drew a small cross, and where he would be in California, he drew another cross. Below the world he included Psalm 139:7-10:

Where can I go from your Spirit? Where can I flee from your presence? If I go up to the heavens, you are there; if I make my bed in the depths, you are there. If I rise on the wings of the dawn, if I settle on the far side of the sea, even there your hand will guide me, your right hand will hold me fast.

George trusted the sentiment that the Lord would be with them and keep them connected even though they were on opposite sides of the world. He felt his gift would help ease the angst that his mother was feeling about him leaving. She graciously accepted the painting and put it where she could see it. He knew that she would be distraught at the airport and braced himself for the comfort he would need to offer her before he boarded the plane. To his surprise, the day George left Scotland, his mother wasn't upset or crying. In fact, she cheerfully hugged him, then waved good-bye and said while smiling, "Enjoy your new adventure, George!"

When George got to the United States, it was a big adventure. He was in a new country, and even though he was settled into his dorm room, he felt lonely in the unfamiliar place among unfamiliar people. He walked to the edge of a cliff overlooking the blue ocean and sat down, mesmerized by the pounding surf, feeling small and almost insignificant. He thought about the gift he had painted for his mom and the verse he had thought would be a comfort to her, but instead it was a comfort to him. In that moment he knew that no matter where he was, even on the far side of the sea, God was with him and had a plan for his life.

He had been surprised that his mom hadn't been more reactive to him leaving. But, in truth, she gave George the greatest gift a mother could ever give her children. George's mother had loved all five of her children and placed herself under the authority of the Lord in raising them to be strong adults. When the time came for George to step to the edge of the nest, spread his wings, and take flight, knowing with full confidence that her job was complete, she moved to the side—not because she didn't care, but because from that point on George would no longer be under his parental authority, but directly under the Lord's.

That is where I think many parents have their biggest struggle—giving up the position we have in our children's lives. The Bible is very clear to honor your father and mother, but it also talks about not having any other God before him.

We want our kids to be under God's direction and leadership, but we still want our foot in the door. Had George's mom not fully relinquished her position, things may have had a different outcome. When George was feeling homesick and lonely, would he have turned to Mom or God? God made the world and all that is in it, but Mom's homemade cookies are a big pull.

If we want our kids to be able to be fully committed to the plans the Lord has for them and be accountable to the Lord, then we need to begin to step away so they will look to the Lord instead of us. They need to be in his direct light—not under our shadow.

TIME TO LET GO

It is always scary to let go of something. I think of how many times as a young girl I would twirl around on the playground bars and then after releasing my grip would rotate through the air and land on my feet. Kids today probably don't even know what a cherry drop is, but we sure did and had the blisters on our palms to prove it. But letting go and trusting that your momentum would carry you through was not always easy, especially if you paused to second-guess yourself.

I think of the trapeze artists who release the hands of someone flying in air, rotate, and grasp the hands of another person who has timed his swing just right. That is kind of how life feels at times—waiting for what we perceive as the perfect time to let go and reach for something else.

Ruth, a friend of ours who came to help out after our sixth child was born, often headed for mission fields and had a heart for proclaiming the gospel to others. When asked how to pray for her, she asked for prayer for the courage to let go of the good to reach for what is great. Wow. How often do we settle for good because it is comfortable, easy, and safe? How often do we encourage our kids to do the same?

"There are two ways that parents raise their kids," stated Annette Spangler, who is on staff at Bayside Church in Granite Bay, California. Annette has several degrees in child development, worked in children's ministry, and teaches parenting classes.

"Parents can either raise their children to be faith-based or fear-based," she said. "A fear-based parenting style results in a safe environment where the kids are always protected and are never really encouraged to venture out into the world. They never fail, because they never attempt anything outside of their comfort zone."

There is a transition time when kids hit high school because they know their time is very short and limited. Some parents hold on tighter and tighter, until the kids are struggling to breathe. It's a bad transition because it becomes more of a flight or fight situation. It is like when a small child reaches out to touch a newly hatched chicken and after touching the soft downy fluff, grasps it with his or her fist so it can't run away. Parents don't intend to cause harm, but that is usually the end result.

"We have to decide if we are going to raise safe kids or strong kids," says Annette. "I don't think God is calling us to raise kids to be safe in their Christian bubble, but to be strong and do the work he has called them to do. We need them to feel confident and trust that God made them and shaped them with a plan and a purpose for their lives."

Annette and her husband have adult sons who are all currently serving the Lord in various ministries. She knows firsthand how difficult it is to have children leave the nest and transition into adult roles, but she encourages other parents to loosen their grip and trust what they have been taught. Let them stretch their wings so that eventually they will be able to soar.

"When my children left home, they did scary things," Annette continued. "One of them went to be a missionary to people leaving the drug trade in Bogota, Colombia. Another one went to war-torn Kosovo to bring God's love and hope to the hurting families. They were not safe, but they were strong in God's mighty power. I had to learn that my boys belonged to God and that I had no choice but to release them. I could do that with grace or not—that was my decision. Was it hard? Yes."

Sometimes letting go doesn't feel very safe, even when we are reaching for something safer.

TOOLS AND TRAINING

If parents haven't been preparing their kids for adulthood, then this time of transition can have added stress, much like someone who hasn't trained getting ready for a triathlon. Putting off taking care of the things that need to be done doesn't delay the starting time. It takes a lot of time and preparation. You have to think ahead and be disciplined with a goal in mind. The same is true with parenting. If parents have been indulgent and have pampered their children during the growing-up years, they will have to evaluate how to get back on track to help launch their child into the world that they have not prepared them for.

Annette strongly suggests parents look into equipping themselves with information on how teens are changing and take advantage of classes or workshops on helping parents communicate better with their teens.

"You need to put tools in your parenting toolbox," said Annette. "It will help you and your teen through this very important time in both of your lives."

WORDS OF WISDOM

For some parents, the act of loosening their grip may take longer than anticipated. The fact that their child is suddenly grown and ready to leave causes many parents to wonder if they have taught them everything they needed to know or encouraged them in the right direction. It is a time of self-reflection for the parents as well as their child.

For some children, leaving the nest right after high school isn't an option. Many students attend junior college and some go to trade schools to use their skills.

Maybe this would be a good time to talk about plans and goals for the future. Children may start their transition with a small step, such as taking on an internship or going on a mission trip. There are many ways to begin taking responsibility to move toward independence.

It's time to let go and get ready to fly.

We can make our plans, but the LORD determines our steps.
Proverbs 16:9, NLT

Reflections

Talk to your child about his or her plans and goals for the future. Write them down in the following pages. In one year, revisit this list with your child. Note areas in which goals have been accomplished, and also note areas in which improvement could be made.

Reflections

Make a list of ways that your child has taken responsibility in his or her life. Encourage your child by sharing this list of achievements with him or her.

12

JUST ME, THE LORD, AND A CONTAINER OF CATERPILLARS

Every time I worked on a chapter, I thought of the many friends and loving family members who have been my encouragers. It has been a journey. I am thankful that for a brief moment we were able to walk it together, you and me.

I want to close with these thoughts. God has a plan, a perfect plan for your life apart from raising your kids. It is like a gift. We can choose to open it or not open it, but it is a gift all the same.

When our kids were all at home I struggled with the thought of them leaving. Face it—I had kids in the eighties, the nineties, and in the first decade of the twenty-first century. Three decades! Being a mom isn't what I do; it is who I am. But God knows how I am made, how you are made, and even the desires of our hearts before we do.

The Lord gave me a precious gift in the silence of our home a few years ago. It was just me, the Lord, and a large container of caterpillars. We had ordered the "caterpillar/butterfly enclosure," complete with a box of caterpillars, from an educational catalog. When it arrived, we set it up in our kitchen nook area so we could watch and record the whole life cycle as part of a science project.

We put food in the clear enclosure as well as twigs and leaves. The caterpillars ate and ate (just like kids do), then grew and grew (just like kids do). Slowly the caterpillars found a nice spot on a twig and planted their feet. They stopped moving. Then they stopped eating and began to harden. Their thick, green, grub-like bodies became colorless and the outer shell became thinner and thinner. In the right light, you could identify traces of wings and an iridescence that almost glowed when the afternoon light came through the nearby window.

One afternoon while all the kids were gone to a church event, I remained home by myself—a rare occurrence. I mulled over the fact that soon the house would always be quiet and empty. And I knew that it really would happen faster than I hoped. The movement of a chrysalis caught my attention. I walked over and looked again. A wiggle. Then another did the same. As if on a command, all five began to slowly rotate.

I have no idea how long I sat there watching, but I just couldn't take my eyes off of what I knew was the moment we had been waiting for. A small slit in the shell opened up as if it were a tiny seam being undone. The light exposed a dark crinkled form that looked like a suit after being shoved in a small suitcase too long. It wiggled and squirmed until free from its constraints. The legs were much longer and delicate. Slowly the rose-petal-shaped appendages began to move. Back and forth. Slowly the tissues fanned open and closed, working simultaneously. The thick body started to thin as fluids were pushed into the now-identifiable and slightly iridescent wings. I marveled as I watched one by one of the butterflies emerge and instinctively completed their transformation. I saw one struggle and resisted the urge to help it along.

"C'mon," I whispered in the silence. "You have come this far!" Despite my best intentions I knew that any assistance would have been detrimental to living to reaching its fullest potential.

Those wormy little leaf crunchers didn't magically turn from one thing into the next. It was evident as we watched the whole journey that everything they needed to be a butterfly really was under the surface all along.

I remember getting choked up. God often uses the small things to make big statements, and at that moment, he had my full attention. I wasn't looking forward to our kids leaving and floating away, but I knew that everything they needed was already inside of them as well. My job wasn't to peel off the layers or try to keep them protected in their chrysalis, but to encourage them and give them what they needed to grow, careful to not crush their newly formed wings when they were ready for flight.

This is a season when our kids are beginning to exchange their childish covering for delicate wings. This is a time of change for us as well. Sometimes I still feel like the large caterpillars that wonder if they are ever going to sip nectar from colorful wildflowers and float on soft summer breezes. Maybe this is a chrysalis time for you—a time to wait and wonder at what will be next. A time to trust that there is life abundant beyond the leaves.

I have written countless articles. What can I say? I have a 750 to 1,200-word attention span. This is my first book project. Proof that God has a sense of humor and uses the least likely for his pleasure, like taking a green grub and releasing it into the sky!

I was the only person, I am sure, in all of Ponderosa High School's history to ever be demoted from the electric typewriter back to manual. When it came to reading, I would rather be doing something else. In English class, when you had to read a certain number of books and write book reports, I would just make something up.

But I always loved stories. I loved hearing them and telling them. I loved seeing how my cousins looked when my grandpa would share stories of tipping over outhouses or hooking the mattress coils to a low-volt battery. I loved the sound of his laugh as it boomed out into the night sky. I loved sitting around a crackling campfire that smelled like cedar kindling, burned Jiffy Pop popcorn kernels, and roasted marshmallows. I loved hearing stories from people who went places I could only dream about. I loved hearing stories about how Jesus took a small boy's lunch and fed the multitudes. Jesus was a storyteller. He always did something creative and genius to make a point.

The Lord wants you to know that no matter how dim your chrysalis time is, he has something in mind. You can trust him with what you have in your lunch tin, even if you wonder how much difference a few loaves and fish will make. He will let you know in some small way that what you marvel about was there all along, like glimpses of butterfly wings under a hard shell.

He took a mom like me, whose first published article was about a baking fiasco of making cookies with our kids, and put it on my heart to write about something that might be heavy on your heart.

I hope in some small way this book has helped encourage you. I hope you know that you are not alone in this parenting adventure and that you know that you are cared for and loved much more than caterpillars.

May the Lord bless your socks off in the days and months ahead and don't forget—the sky is *not* the limit for you or your kids, so fan your wings, take flight, and let the journey continue!

NOTES

Chapter 7

1. Marcia Reynolds, "Wander Woman: How High-Achieving Women Find Contentment and Direction," *Huffington Post* (March 10, 2010).

Chapter 8

1. Erica Ho, "Survey: 85% of New College Grads Move Back in with Mom and Dad," *Time Magazine* (May 10, 2011).

2. Linda Perlman Gordon, "The Money Question: Budgeting for Your Adult Children," *Ladies' Home Journal*, no. 7 (March 2013).

Chapter 10

1. Melinda Smith and Jeanne Segal, "Coping with Grief and Loss," http://www.helpguide.org/mental/grief_loss.htm .

2. Kathryn Roethel, "Antidepressants—Nation's Top Prescription," *San Francisco Chronicle* (November 13, 2012).

Chapter 12

1. C. McNair Wilson, *Hatch! Brainstorming Secrets of a Theme Park Designer* (Colorado Springs: Book Villages, 2012), 26.

About the Author

Marci Seither's writing career begin after her family humor article was published in the small-town newspaper.

Since then she has authored two books and hundreds of articles for local papers as well as contributing to national publications such as Guideposts, Light & Life, and Focus On The Family and is always working on new projects.

She loves to teach creative brainstorming at writers conferences. When asked if she had always wanted to be a writer, her response is, "No, but I have always loved being a storyteller."

Marci has been married to John for over 35 years. They currently live in California with their youngest son and a very animated mini-schnauzer named Pepper.

You can find out more about Marci by following her at www.MarciSeither.com.

Made in the USA
Monee, IL
25 August 2020

Reflections

When have you been tempted to step in and help your child when he needed to handle something on his own? List a few areas that you may need to work on.

_____

_____

_____

_____

_____

_____

_____

_____

_____

_____

_____

_____

_____